BUSINESS ISSUES, COMPETITION AND ENTREPRENEURSHIP

FINANCIAL CRISIS AND ADVENTURES OF THE GEORGIAN LARI

BUSINESS ISSUES, COMPETITION AND ENTREPRENEURSHIP

Additional books in this series can be found on Nova's website under the Series tab.

Additional e-books in this series can be found on Nova's website under the e-books tab.

BUSINESS ISSUES, COMPETITION AND ENTREPRENEURSHIP

FINANCIAL CRISIS AND ADVENTURES OF THE GEORGIAN LARI

LAMARA QOQIAURI

NOVINKA

New York

Library of Congress Cataloging-in-Publication Data

Names: Qoqiauri, Lamara, author.
Title: Financial crisis and adventures of the Georgian lari / Lamara Qoqiauri.
Description: Hauppauge, New York : Nova Science Publishers, Inc., [2016] |
Series: Business issues, competition and entrepreneurship | Includes
bibliographical references and index.
Identifiers: LCCN 2016004818 (print) | LCCN 2016012391 (ebook) | ISBN
9781634847834 (softcover) | ISBN 9781634847964 ()
Subjects: LCSH: Foreign exchange--Georgia (Republic) | Financial
crises--Georgia (Republic) | Money--Georgia (Republic) | Georgia
(Republic)--Economic policy.
Classification: LCC HG3968.24 .Q67 2016 (print) | LCC HG3968.24 (ebook) | DDC
332.4/94758--dc23
LC record available at http://lccn.loc.gov/2016004818

Published by Nova Science Publishers, Inc. † New York

CONTENTS

Foreword **vii**
Iasha Meskhia

Introduction **ix**

Chapter 1 When and Why the Drop in the Exchange Rate of Georgian Lari Began? **1**

Chapter 2 What Gives Rise to the Deepening Tax Deficit? **11**

Chapter 3 Does Foreign Debt Influence the Exchange Rate of Georgian Lari? **25**

Chapter 4 What Are Outcomes of Georgian Lari and Whose Fault Is It? **31**

Chapter 5 How Fiscal Policy Influenced Changes in the Rates of Georgian Lari **37**

Chapter 6 What Shall We Do to Save Georgian Lari and the Georgian Economy?! **43**

Chapter 7 Brief History of Origination of Georgian Money **61**

Summarizing Opinions **93**

Conclusion **103**

Appendix 1. Everybody Shall Work Together **107**

Appendix 2. Samples of Georgian Money in Different Eras **109**

References **117**

About the Author **121**

Index **123**

FOREWORD

The Monograph of the Doctor of Economics, Professor Lamara Qoqiauri "Financial Crisis and Adventure of Georgian Lari" is the research of original nature dedicated to actual theoretical, practical and historical issues of the Georgian monetary unit. Today, as never before in Georgia, it became necessary to learn current changes in the economy of the country, identification and elimination of the objective and subjective reasons giving rise to the sharp fall of the exchange rate of Georgian Lari, selection of extreme situations created in the country and prevention of expected inflation, developing reliable facilities and sources for saving the national currency.

The Purpose of the Author is to develop recommendations for root cause analysis, substantiation of inevitability of Devaluation of Georgian Lari, developing correct monetary and fiscal policy, regulation of the Lari exchange rate, extending the economy of the country, increasing foreign investments, creating an attractive investment climate and activation of large investment projects, raising potential exports and improvement of the incentives.

Excitement in connection with the National Currency taking place in Georgia during recent years caught the interest of Georgian scientists and economists in the faith of the national currency of the country – Lari; multiple articles have been written and published, important versions to stop devaluation and expected inflation of Lari appeared.

Complexity, severity, versatility, necessity and possibilities of their solutions towards saving and improving Georgian money, again in the area of my scientific research.

Purpose and tasks of the Manuscript determined its architectonics and the following sequence of issues:

Introduction; 1) When and Why the Drop in the Exchange Rate of Georgian Lari Began? 2) What Gives Rise to the Deepening Tax Deficit? 3) Does Foreign Debt Influence the Exchange Rate of Georgian Lari? 4) What are Outcomes of Georgian Lari and Whose Fault Is It? 5) How Fiscal Policy of Government has Influenced the Changing Exchange Rate of Lari? 6) What Can We Do to Save Georgian Lari and Georgian Economy?! 6) a. Growth of Real Sector of Economy – Main Means for Exchange Adjustment; 6) b. To Make Investment Climate More Attractive to Local and Foreign Investors; 6) c. Monetary and Fiscal Policy shall Together Serve the Restoration of the Georgian Lari; 6) d. Inflation Expectations, Monetary Speculations and New Economic Dangers; 7) Brief History Notes of the Origin of Georgian Money;

Due to the fact that the Monograph is written in English and in case of its publishing, I considered it necessary to attach brief historic chronicles and illustrations of the National Currency of Georgia.

Results of the study are represented in the Monograph in the form of 10 economic axioms of solving problems. Their implementation will support general sustainability of economy, correct management of monetary and fiscal policy of the country, and improvement of attractiveness of investment climate, etc. For illustration, the book is attached with charts, tables, and samples of ancient Georgian money and a bibliography.

Iasha Meskhia, Professor
President of the Georgian Academy of Economic Sciences
and Doctor of Economic Science

INTRODUCTION

I have refrained myself from writing the present manuscript for a long period of time. I think I tried to avoid hasty conclusions. I had to review theoretical and classic issues of cash flow, inflation, monetary-credit policy here in Georgia, as in other developed and developing countries.

I have many questions:

- Was the drop in the exchange rate of the Georgian Lari inevitable and necessary?
- Are we afraid of recognition of extremely serious changes in the economy – when transformation of the market-oriented economy into the social oriented one takes place?
- Is it time for determining the exchange rate of the National Currency at the open market?
- Has it finally been determined if the drop in the exchange rate of Georgian Lari, which started at the end of 2013, is inflation or devaluation?
- Why don't we, the economists, speak more openly and boldly and explain the role of using the factor of foreign debt in non-maintenance of the exchange rate of Georgian Lari?
- Why are we looking for the reasons of devaluation of Georgian Lari in subjective factors? If the National Bank has made mistakes in maintenance-non-maintenance of the "sharp" drop in the exchange rate, is it the mistake of others? And generally, should we mention the fault – in the course of solving or not solving the economic fate of the country?

- I'd prefer to ask one simple question instead of those named above – how can we rescue the Georgian Lari, Economy, my people, and my country? What shall we do?

The problem is topical. It is immediately necessary to learn the changes taking place in the economy of the Country, as well as identification and elimination of objective and subjective reasons of the drop in the exchange rate of Georgian Lari (and not shifting responsibilities and sometimes ungrounded blaming of others).

My great teachers, the Academicians Vasil Chantladze and Paata Gugushvili, among others, used to give wise counsel: science is not in need of party status; only education, reasonableness, knowledge and experience shall be involved here.

Georgia has always had and fortunately has educated economists, professors: Merab Kakulia, Nodar Chitanava, Roman Gotsiridze, Nana Aslamazishvili, Irakli Kovzanadze, Elguja Meqvabishvili, Ioseb Archvadze, Iakob Meskhia, Lia Eliava, the Academicians Avtandil Silagadze, Vladimer Papava, and many others, and our young talented economists. All these, who are capable and responsible for leading and healing the Georgian economy, along with termination and avoidance of created extreme situation; we shall get together, invert, outline, and develop reliable means and methods of saving the Georgian Lari.

Though it is not late …

In the course of our research, we were based exactly on the thinking of the above Georgian researchers and economists, data of international organizations, materials of periodicals, National Service of Statistics of Georgia, and materials of National Bank of Georgia, World Bank, International Monetary Fund, Investment Partnership Fund of Georgia and other organizations.

And to my mind, the main thing is that we are not looking for the means of solving the problems, where we see them. It's time to develop, name and protect axioms of economic development: sustainable growth of the economy, immediate development of industry, agriculture and processing industry, and development of small, middle and other businesses for the country and people; it's time, if not too late, to open small, middle and large delivery and processing enterprises in every town and every region of Georgia (this will not take place without involvement of the Government) to avoid spoiling tons of fruit, vegetables, greens, citruses, and grapes of Georgian farmers.

Moreover, Georgian wheat, grape, citrus, barley, and corn shall be receipted by the government or it shall support the supply receivers to let its people eat healthy bread; not to drink chemically treated juice, but natural ones; not to feed our cattle with combined food rejected in other countries, but prepare and feed them with ours.

Going back to our main topic, we shall recognize that the National bank did not devaluate the Lari, but decades of non-development of material industry (as it is today called 'real sector of economy' L.Q.). (They will call me Marxist…by the way; economists of our generation were grown on Marx's Capital. I don't keep it from you!), and the passive nature of the production sector devaluated national Lari. Only trading, service fields, infrastructure, construction of houses, and a wide network of hotels and catering units will save the economy of the country; innovative ways of economic development are necessary, as well as an investment boom, for creation of a favorable, attractive investment environment for investors; processing and implementation of correct fiscal policy; creation of a reliable, legal (!) and legislative framework of invariable nature bounding and identical to everybody; to delete hostility, contentiousness; everybody shall do his work: politicians shall take care of the policy, the economy shall be managed by economists; ill persons shall be cured by the physician; scientists shall learn and teach, write works, books; legislators shall write laws and legalize them(!); farmers shall harvest crops; manufacturers shall produce; the government shall protect the interests of people and country…, etc. The list is too long.

I will do my bit and continue working.

Thus, the purpose of my manuscript has been revealed:

- Cause-consequence analysis of depreciation of national currency, at the background of certifying inevitability of devaluation of Georgian Lari, for development of correct monetary and fiscal policy, regulation of exchange rate of Georgian Lari, economic growth in the country, increasing foreign investment flow for creation of an attractive investment climate and activation of large investment projects, development of recommendations for increasing export potential and improvement of promotion mechanisms.

In the course of working on the manuscript we were greatly assisted with the researches of Georgian scientists, analytical data of economic experts, regulatory and statistic documentation of Georgian and foreign central banks, official data of the National Service of Statistics of Georgia (Saqstati), data of the National Bank of Georgia, World Bank, International Monetary Fund, data of international organizations, International Partnership Fund of Georgia and other international organizations, as well as popular articles published in the central media of the country.

We are also grateful to R. Gotsiridze, I. Archvadze, N. Javakhishvili, M. Kakulia, R. Kakulia, I. Meskhia, T. Basilia, A. Sadikovi, N. Chichinadze, L. Eliava, S. Pavliashvili, L. Martadze, V. Khomizurashvili, M. Griffith, A. Silagadze, M. Tokmajishvili, I. Kovzanadze, L. Qistauri, L. Kalandadze, B. Manchadze, I. Gharibashvili, N. Aslamazashvili, M. Skhirtladze, O. Anguridze, I. Doghonadze, G. Charaia, P. Bairakhar, V. Khomizurashvili, B. Danelia, O. Torabelidze, Sh. Gulbani, A. Beglarishvili, E. Tukhiashvili, G. Shagidze, Z. Kukuladze, N. Khaduri, M. Tsomaia, E. Abzianidze, E. Mgaloblishvili, T. Keinashvili, with direct and indirect support of whom we were able to complete the work process and submission of our modest manuscript.

The author of the Manuscript would be pleased to receive each useful and constructive remark to the email: lqoqiauri@yahoo.com; tel.: +995 599 90-60-11.

ABSTRACT

Financial Crisis and Adventures of the Georgian Lari is original research, which is dedicated to the solution of the theoretical and practical issues of Georgian monetary unit –Lari. The topic is actual, as today as never before it has become essential to research current changes in the economy of Georgia, and to identify and eliminate subjective and objective reasons for decreasing the Georgian national currency.

Thus, it is my duty as well as the duty of Georgian economists to eliminate the extreme situation in the country, avoid inflation of the Georgian Lari and process non-alternative means for Lari's survival.

According to my personal opinion, the non-alternative way to solve the problems faced by the country is sustainable growth of the Georgian economy as a whole, acute development of the real sector as well as small and middle businesses. There is a need for the development of the innovative way of country's economy, investment boom, creation of a favorable, attractive investment environment for investors, processing and implementation of a correct fiscal economy, improvement of increasing export potential and promotion of their mechanisms.

The principle audience for the publication is: students, graduates, doctoral students in the field of economy, high school and college professors and teachers; representatives of financial and banking fields; also workers related with the foreign exchange operations and currency.

Keywords: financial crisis, Georgian Lari, axiom, monetary, economy, inflation, devaluation

Chapter 1

When and Why the Drop in the Exchange Rate of Georgian Lari Began?

From theoretical perspective – there is a direct and reverse relation between monetary relations and reproduction process. Objective grounds for monetary relations are processes of such pubic reproduction, which give rise to an international exchange of goods, money and labor.

Development of monetary relations significantly depends on development of the national and global economy, as well as relations formed between the political situation and different countries of the world.

We take into account the fact that international relations, including monetary ones, are in close relation with such fields, as policy, economy, diplomacy, commerce, industrial production and trading, and occupy an important place in the national and global economy. Settlement, credit, and financial operations implemented between different countries and their economic subjects give rise to transformation of national currency into foreign currencies and vice-versa.

Under the conditions of globalization of industrial relations, dependence of the reproduction process upon such foreign factors as: international trade, export-import operations and production development, as well as foreign currency circulation, etc. are getting stronger. Instable state of international currency relations and monetary crisis may negatively influence the reproduction process.

Let us consider it from top down. To my mind, Devaluation of the Georgian Lari started in the year 2013; the second wave was in 2014, and the third wave in 2015, i.e., devaluation of thc Georgian Lari began two years ago and continues today.

Before speaking about reasons for devaluation of Georgian Lari, I consider it necessary to note that the long-term target rate of inflation of the national bank is 3 percent. Taking into account the fact that today Georgia is among developing countries, and the economy is characterized in a higher rate of inflation and economic growth, targeted inflation according to the documents of monetary-credit line for the years 2015-2016 is determined to be 5 percent, which will be decreased to 4 percent for the year 2017 [1, pg. 8].

After deflation processes were fixed in 2012-2013, the trend of increasing rate of inflation was fixed from 2014, though it is maintained lower than the target rate of the National Bank of Georgia. Reduced prices and the fall of oil prices in the commodity market greatly influenced the dynamics of prices. This was accompanied by the weakening of foreign demand. In April 2015, the index of total inflation was 2.5%, which was mostly conditioned by the fact that at the background of depreciation of the exchange rate of Georgian Lari, the influence of the growth of intermediary costs related with the service of denominated loans with foreign currency upon inflation was partially balanced with reduction of prices on fuel.

According to existed evaluation, in the first quarter economic growth was higher than expected level. With preliminary information, in the first quarter real growth was 3.2 percent. Credit assets in the first quarter were moderately increased by an important slowdown in April. Besides this, the expected slowdown of April imports may indicate reduction of demand. By means of development of foreign shocks, negative trends were fixed in the foreign sector. At the background of the deteriorated economic situation in commercial partner states, from the second quarter of 2014, trends of reducing foreign demands were identified and they gradually strengthened. The volume of exports registered in the first quarter was reduced 28 percent, and imports 3 percent. Significant decrease was fixed in the index of money transfers: it was reduced by 23.5 percent per annum in March. Since the year 2014, the rate of increasing tourist incomes decreased significantly. Though the last change of exchange rate gave rise to the reflection on the import demand, which, in its turn, provide elimination of foreign imbalance and supporting local demand.

During this period, the National bank extracted US Dollars from the economy and released Georgian Lari. Until November of 2013, the National Bank of Georgia purchased up to 555 million US Dollars, i.e., before depreciation of the Georgian Lari, it extracted from the economy the sum of the same amount and released Lari of respective amount in exchange.

In December of 2014, when trading was enhanced from the point of import and when demand on the US Dollar increased, the first strong wave of devaluation was started.

During this period, the National Bank of Georgia returned US Dollars to the economy in small portions and it returned 220 million US Dollars in two months. Distinction is significant.

Justification– when National Bank of Georgia was receiving US Dollars from the economy, it gave explanations that it was doing that for avoidance of danger of excess stability of the Georgian Lari and filling currency reserves.

At the same time, inflation was quietly "ripening." Operating business-companies didn't increase prices at the beginning and were waiting for stability of the exchange rate of Georgian Lari. After disappointment, prices first started increasing "invisibly" and later – "visibly."

Two years ago – in 2009-2010, in 18 months the National Bank of Georgia provided the economy with 450 Million US Dollars and reduced currency reserved to 1.9 billion US Dollars. Today currency reserve is 2.6 billion US Dollars. For sustainability of the financial system, it is necessary to have a volume of reserves more than triple the amount of imports, totaling up to 1.7 billion US Dollars.

Conclusion: The National Bank of Georgia has had more than enough reserves.

This argument doesn't greatly differ from the opinion of the ex-president of the National Bank of Georgia: "according to the standard determined by the International Monetary Fund, currency reserves shall be the same amount as triple volume of the average one month import. This is about 1.8 billion. At the same time the volume of currency reserves is about 2.5 billion, i.e., it was easy to do something" [2].

Global economic activity was characterized by important fluctuations in 2014, the trend of reduction prices on the main trading commodity products (oil, food, metals) at the international markets, strengthened geopolitical crisis and hard heritage of global financial crisis influenced essentially by economies of developed, increasing and developing countries. High levels of unemployment are still maintained in many countries of the euro region, as well as the negative attitude of investors and structural problems, reflected in the less than expected level of economic growth. Less than expected economic growth was detected in Japan, where at the background of weakened foreign demand and increased payments, monetary softening implemented by the Central Bank appeared to be insufficient for improvement of consuming and business moods. There was a much better situation in the USA and United

Kingdom, which was supported by softened monctary policy and increasing investments in the real estate market. Economic perspective of increasing and developing trade partners of Georgia was worsened in 2014 – subject to the geopolitical crisis in Russia and Ukraine and accompanying economic outcomes. According to the evaluation of International Monetary Fund (IMF), the global economic growth of 2014 equaled 3.3 percent, which is scarcely different from the rate of 2013** (see the Chart No. 1). As for the prognosis, in the years 2015 and 2016, the global economy increased by 3.5 and 3.7 percent, respectively.

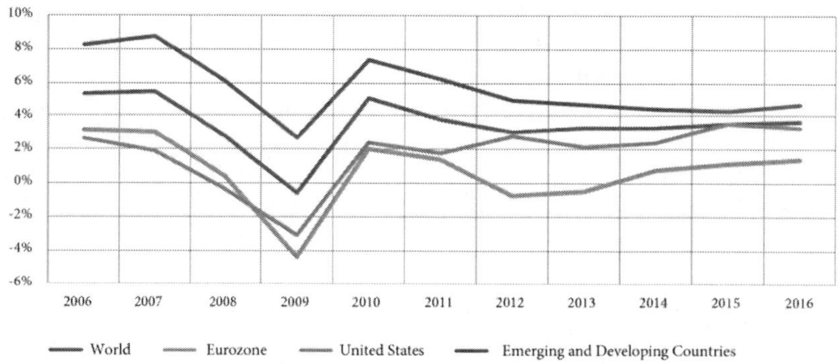

**Source: International Monetary Fund, WEO Update, Jan-2015.

Chart 1. Real Growth of Gross Domestic Product in the World.

Trend of reducing prices on the main trading commodity products (oil, food, metals) at international markets and the negative gap of issuance conditions weakened inflation in many countries (See the Chart no. 2.). In the second part of 2014, prices on Brent Crude were radically decreased – from 150 US Dollars to 55 US Dollars per barrel. There are several reasons causing this reduction. In the first place, the effect of supply is higher than expected and the background of weakened global demand is noteworthy, which, in its turn, conditioned increase rate of shale oil production in the USA. This was accompanied by two additional factors: the decision of OPEC member states not to alienate market share (at the expense of sharp cutting of sale price and stabilization of US Dollars in relation with other currencies (which, of course, additionally reduces demand on oil in the countries importing energy).

In 2014, important reduction in prices was detected under the conditions of excess supply, even on the most tradable foods (corn, sugar, dairy products, soy), conditioned by favorable climate situations and reduction of intermediary expenditures. Prices of metals were also characterized with the trend of reduction, subject to the reduced demand on raw materials in the economy of China and other countries of increasing economies (see Chart 3).

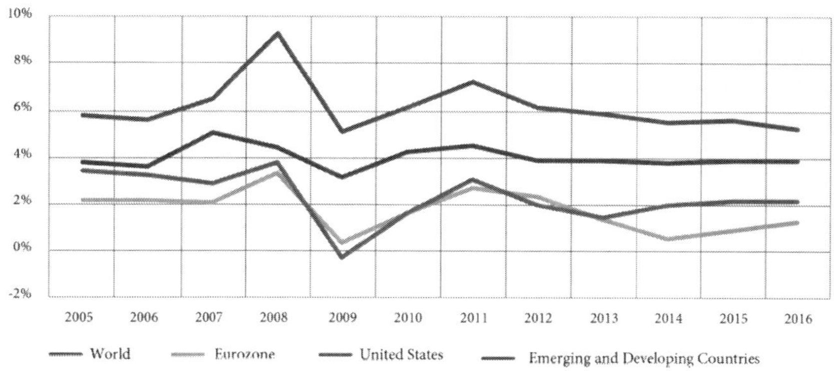

Source: International Monetary Fund.

Chart 2. Consumer Price Index in the world.

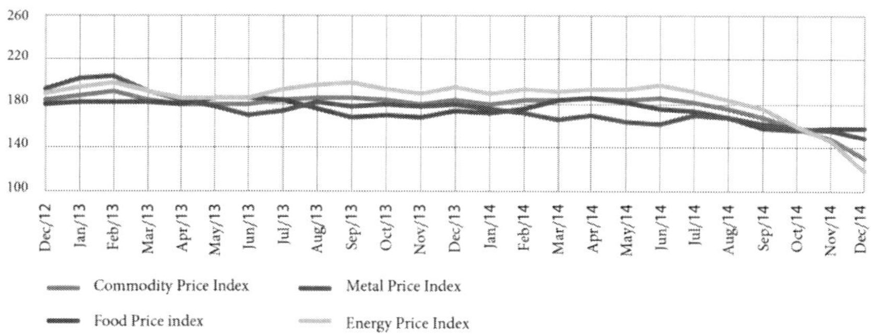

Source: International Monetary Fund.

Chart 3. Price Rates of Main Commodity Products, 2005 = 100.

Gross Domestic Product of the USA increased far more than expected at 2.4 percent. Growth of economic activity was conditioned with softened monetary and fiscal policy, which was attended by a recovering real estate market and increase of real incomes increased by means of reducing oil prices. The level of unemployment was significantly reduced (about 6 percent), creating grounds for leaving the phase of monetary softening. Although, by means of reducing oil price and strengthening US Dollars, inflation at end of year conditions slowed and staged the nature of the tightening policy. According to the International monetary Fund in 2015-2016, the US economy increased by 3.6 and 3.3 percent respectively [3].

In 2014, in many countries of the euro region, a high level of unemployment is maintained, as well as negative expectations of investors and structural problems. Gross domestic product of the unified monetary zone increased only 0.8 percent, which was conditioned with real economic growth less than expected in France, Germany and Italy. Still, an unstable political and economic situation persisted in Greece, though, in other countries of Europe, namely in Spain and Ireland, there are clear signs of improvement. Inflation of the euro region, with the influence of weak demand and reduction of oil prices, was maintained on a lower level than targeted, even in 2014. According to the prognosis of the International Monetary Fund, GDP of the Euro Region in 2015 increased by 1.2 percent, and in 2016 – by 1.4 percent [4].

Geopolitical conflict between Ukraine and Russia and accompanying economic outcomes, create negative perspective for the growth of issuance for these countries and other important trade partners of Georgia. Economic sanctions against Russia at the end of 2014 were added with the reduction of the global price on oil, which appeared to be hard stress for the export-oriented economy of energy-carriers. Worsening trade conditions could not compensate for devaluation in 85 percent of Russian Ruble against US Dollars. In exchange, devaluation was reflected in high inflation and reduced real incomes, which had a significantly negative influence upon export of foreign countries and cash transfers from Russia. Maintenance of negative trends is expected in the near future – with the most optimistic assessment, that the GDP of Russia in 2015 will be reduced about 3-5 percent [5].

As for the Ukraine, the economy of the Country was reduced about 8 percent in 2014; and local currency was devaluated by 98 percent against US Dollars. Based on entering a new phase of military conflict, conflict in the Ukraine is expected to enter into extensive recession and Gross Domestic Product in 2015 will be increased by 5 percent [6].

The outlook for Armenia, an important trade partner of Georgia increased as well, which was mainly conditioned with close economic relations with Russia and expressed in devaluation of local currency against US Dollars by 17 percent and essential reduction of cash transfers from Russia. According to the existed prognosis [7], in 2015 the economy of Armenia will have zero-percent growth. Problems existing in the region are reflected on the economy of Azerbaijan, though, for the countries exporting energy, reduction of global prices on oil became very important, which worsened the perspective of economic growth of 2015. At the regional level, relatively better perspective was identified in Turkey, where in 2014 the economy increased 2.9 percent. With the existed prognosis, growth of GDP of Turkey in 2015 will be 3.0 percent [8].

For handling inflation risks, central banks of the region pursued strict monetary policy in 2014 – in the case of Russia and the Ukraine, principle rate of policy at the end of the year were 17 and 14 percent, relatively. A radically different situation is maintained in the euro zone, where the purpose of the Central bank remained to be maximal alleviation of credit conditions for the purpose of promotion of demand and investments. Similarly, in the United States of America, they maintained an alleviated monetary policy, notwithstanding declaration of the Federal Reserve System on leaving the soft monetary policy.

At the background of the foreign shocks described above, we shall also pay attention to the circumstances developed at the monetary market. Parallel to the positive economic trends and expectations taking place in the USA, since the end of 2013 the Federal Reserve System started reduction of quantitative alleviation and finally in October of 2014 it made a decision about its completion. At the background of the said circumstances, the US Dollar starts appreciation. Consequently, from the beginning of 2014, world currencies were significantly devaluated against the US Dollar. Influence of these processes was reflected later (at the end of the year) on the exchange rate of the Georgian Lari, as during the first three quarters they fixed moderate inflow of foreign currencies into the country. It shall also be noted that appreciation of the US Dollar was reflected in the first place on the currencies of such countries, where there is a more developed financial market. This process was transferred to Georgia later, by means of devaluation of the currencies of partner countries by worsening the currency account of tax balance (deepening trade deficit of goods, reduction of cash transfers and the slowdown of increasing tourist incomes).

Expressed negative trends gave rise to backwardness of the economy from its potential level, retarding the approach of the inflation index with the target index and extending the process of leaving an alleviated monetary policy.

Thus, so-called “external factors” influencing the exchange rate of Georgian Lari, and the global phenomenon described above, are of long-term and unavoidable nature. Due to this, Georgian Lari “behaved” adequately; it would be more surprising if the rate had not suffered changes. It was impossible to avoid devaluation of the Georgian Lari.

In each of Georgia's trading partner states, sharp devaluation of national currencies took place against the US Dollar.

Negative balance of export-import of Georgia made 5735.07 million US Dollars (export – 2861.19 million US Dollars, import – 8596.26 million US Dollars) in 2014. The top ten largest countries were as follows: Azerbaijan – 19 percent, Armenia – 10 percent, Russia – 10 percent, Turkey – 8 percent, USA – 7 percent, Bulgaria – 6 percent, Ukraine - 5 percent, China – 3 percent, Kazakhstan – 3 percent, Italy – 3 percent, and others 26 percent.

As you can see, Azerbaijan is the leader in exports of Georgia, almost twice those of Armenia and Russia (occupying 2nd and 3rd positions respectively). The top ten importing countries are importantly different, where Turkey is the absolute leader during several years. Imports to Georgia in 2014 were as follows: Turkey – 20 percent, China – 9 percent, Azerbaijan – 7 percent, Ukraine – 6 percent, Germany – 5 percent, Japan – 4 percent, Romania – 4 percent, USA – 3 percent, Italy – 3 percent, all others – 32 percent. We have distinguished the 12 largest trading partner countries, economies of which influence the exchange rate of Georgian Lari. In Table 1 below, we represent indexes of export-import of these countries in monetary and percentage sections.

What happens in the countries from the point of devaluation of national currencies is very interesting. If we take last 2 years for reporting period, it appears that the Turkish Lira was devalued 44.8% since January 2012 till today, and during last 4 months – about 20%. Though, the Chinese Yuan has been formed in the world to be one of the strongest monetary units, the trend of appreciation of US Dollar during last period has been reflected on it and it was devalued in 4.6%. By means of monetary policy pursued in Azerbaijan, Manat was devaluated in 33% in February this year. To be more precise, the government was maintaining exchange rate of national currency artificially and when it made decision not to be involved, Manat "jumped" in 31% in one day. Today Azerbaijan is continuing control of the rate in order to avoid currency manipulations.

Let us consider separately the fortune of Russian and Ukrainian national currencies.

- Indexes of Russia and Ukraine are catastrophic. These countries are equivalent trade partners to Georgia. Ruble in Russia was devalued against US Dollars in 144.4% from the year 2012, and during last 4 months the fall was 85%. As for the Ukrainian Hryvnia, it was devalued 4.2 after January of 2012 till today, and during the last period at the background of current political circumstances – 2.8 times.

Table 1. Indexes of export-import of the trading partner countries of Georgia in monetary and percentage section; year 2014

No.	Name	Import 2014		Export 2014		Balance 2014
		Million USD	%	Million USD	%	
1	Turkey	1727,42	20,10	239,31	8,36	-1488,11
2	China	732,96	8,53	90,39	3,16	-642,57
3	Azerbaijan	637,59	7,42	544,42	19,03	-93,17
4	Russia	577,71	6,72	274,96	9,61	-302,75
5	Ukraine	546,14	6,35	140,21	4,90	-405,92
6	Germany	465,85	5,42	69,14	2,42	-396,71
7	Japan	368,17	4,28	3,28	0,11	-364,89
8	Romania	311,40	3,62	4,03	0,14	-307,37
9	USA	287,39	3,34	207,58	7,26	-79,81
10	Italy	221,62	2,58	86,19	3,01	-135,43
11	Armenia	210,31	2,45	288,24	10,07	77,93
12	Bulgaria	209,77	2,44	164,09	5,74	-45,68
	Others	2299,92	26,75	749,32	26,19	-1550,60
	Total	8596,26	100,00	2861,19	100,00	-5735,07

Source: Data of the National Bank of Georgia.

The rating of the largest trading partner countries of Georgia from the euro region included Italy and Germany.

As we can see, the Euro was depreciated 25% after May, 2014. Japanese Yen was devalued 62.5% against US Dollars during last 2 years, and 15% during last period. We can find similar situation in fluctuations of national currencies of Romania and Bulgaria. This proves the fact of effect of economic situation over neighboring countries. Armenian Drums was distinguished in particular stability since 2012, but during the last 4 months, it could not avoid depreciation of 17%.

With this background Georgian Lari is as follows:

Looking deeper into the content, we will see similar notes with Russian Ruble, Ukrainian Hryvnia and Armenian Drum. In the numerical index, there is similarity with Turkey. Particularly, over 2 years Georgian Lari and Turkish Lira was devalued within the bounds of 43-44%. The distinction is that the process is being provided gradually from 2013. As for Georgia, devaluation of Georgian Lari was being prepared “quietly,” and the sharp drop began at the end of 2014. This is why this impacted the population so painfully.

Georgia is in close relation with economic circumstances of Turkey, Azerbaijan, Russia and Ukraine. At the same time, the EU Association Agreement will soon be fully validated fully. We shall assume that the Georgian Lari depends and will depend on the conduct of national currencies of the above states and devaluation of national currencies in their neighbor countries will be continued, and adequate conduct of Georgian Lari will be inevitable.

As for the consumer prices, according to the largest importer countries, we may analyze: to our mind, prices on Chinese goods will definitely be increased about 15-20%; a rise in prices on Ukrainian and Russian products shall not be more than 5% and on the contrary, if military actions will be continued, they may become even cheaper; prices for the goods imported from the euro region and Turkey will increase about 10-15%. As for the energy carriers, at the current stage it is impossible to predict the increase of prices, though the main concern of the Government of Georgia will be maintenance of price on energy carriers through negotiations with Azerbaijan until stabilization of the existed situation; otherwise crash of the Georgian economy will be inevitable.

Herewith, one of the main factors for devaluation of national currency is the outcome of political-economic processes of the neighbor states. Opposition to devaluation of Georgian Lari would be counter-productive, having temporary effect.

Chapter 2

What Gives Rise to the Deepening Tax Deficit?

The tax balance is an important strategic account reflecting economic operations implemented between countries and the rest of the world. It reflects masses of currency entering and leaving the country.

The 2014 deficit report was 9.7 percent of Gross Domestic Product, which is more than 4.0 percentage points of that index in the previous year. The deficit in the current report in absolute dimension was deeper in 681 million US Dollars and made 1.6 billion US Dollars. In 2014, parallel to the growth of local demand in comparison with year preceding 2014, deepening of the deficit of the current account was expected, although foreign shocks eliminated in the second half of 2014 supported deepening of the deficit of current account.

The deepening deficit of 2014 is mostly conditioned with a worsening trade balance. Conformity of the deficit of trading goods with Gross Domestic Product was 25.6 percent, which is higher than the index of the previous year by 3.9 percentage points. In the absolute image, deficit of trading goods in 2014 worsened by 733 million US Dollars. It is noteworthy that growth of deficit of trading goods during the year was unequal. 35.8 percent of the trading goods deficit came at the first part of the year, and 64.2 percent in the second part of the year. Sharp worsening of the trade deficit in the second part of 2014 was conditioned by the crisis situation developed in the main trading partner countries of Georgia, which was reflected negatively on the Georgian export. In the first part of 2014, export of goods and services increased by 7.4 percent per annum. During the same period, import of goods and services increased 13.4 percent. In the second part, import of goods and services continued growth (+2.4 percent), while during the said period the export was reduced 8.6 percent, which gave rise to the sharp worsening of the deficit of trading goods and services in the second part of the year.

During 2014, compared with the previous years incomes made from the trading service was reduced by 4.6 percent totaling 1.34 billion US Dollars. In 2014, reduction of incomes of this type were mostly conditioned on the deceasing rate of tourist inflow, therefore worsening the balance of trading transport service. Tourist income, the principle part of export of services, was 1.79 billion US Dollars in 2014, which is more than the index of the previous year at 3.9 percent.

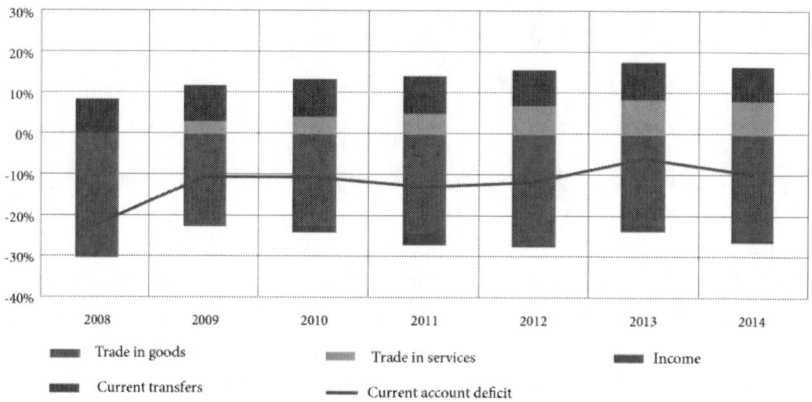

Source: National Bank of Georgia.

Chart 4. Conformity of the components of current account with the GDP.

Conformity of tourist income in 2014 with the GDP was 10.8 percent, which is higher compared with the index of previous year by 0.2 percentage points. Reduction of the rate of growth of tourist inflows caused the low growth rate of the number of visitors (1.9 percent), which was mostly because of a reduction in the number of visitors from Turkey (-10.1 percent). Reduction of the amount of visitors was especially expressed in the fourth quarter of 2014, when the reduction of visitors was fixed from Ukraine (-11 percent), from Poland (-23 percent) and from Iran (-81 percent). In the same period, compared with the previous year, the amount of visitors entering from Russia remained relatively unchanged, which finally gave rise to the reduction of the rate of growth of tourist influence.

In 2014, income was slightly improved, though it was still deficit. In 2014, deficit of investment incomes was improved by 12.5 percent and made 821.3 million US Dollars, though, notwithstanding improvement, it remains to be the largest negative component of the account of incomes. Herewith, in 2014 the balance of remuneration of workers improved 5.1 percent per annum and made 662.8 million US Dollars. Consequently, deficit of the account of income compared with the year 2014 was improved significantly and it made 158.5 million US Dollars.

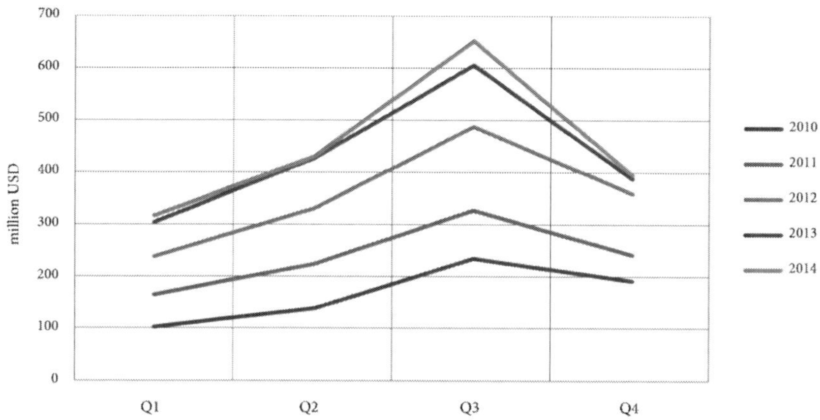

Source: National Bank of Georgia.

Chart 5. Incomes made from export of tourism (2010-2014).

Net profit made in the form of current transfers, which occupies an important share together with tourist inflows in funding the trade deficit, was reduced by 2.3 percent per annum during the year 2014 and made 1.43 billion US Dollars. The transfers, making largest component current transfers, was reduced by 3.2 percent and made 1.43 billion US Dollars. Reduction of transfers was identified in the fourth quarter of 2014, when due to the circumstances developed in Russia and Ukraine worker transfers were reduced 15.1 percent.

The main source of funding the 2014 deficit, similar to previous years, was represented by direct foreign investments. Direct foreign investments in Georgia created 1.3 billion US Dollars in 2014, which is more than the previous year index by 34.8 percent. Growth of direct foreign investments was greatly conditioned by the growth of investments in the construction sector. Compared to the year 2013, direct foreign investments in the said sector were increased almost 5 times, mostly related with construction in preparation for the Youth Olympics. In 2014, investments in the sectors of transport and communication (+145 percent), real estate (+106 percent), processing industry (+74.5 percent) and agriculture (+61 percent) were significantly increased. In 2014, direct investments entered from EU countries increased 64 percent creating 640.5 million US Dollars. Growth in investments was mostly conditioned with the growth of investments from the Netherlands and Great Britain. Investments from the CIS states made 353.0 million US Dollars, which is more than the index of previous year by 168 percent. Growth of investments from CIS countries was mostly because of the growth of investments from Azerbaijan (+269 percent). Growth of the volume of investments from Azerbaijan was mostly related with the investment into the construction of a new pipeline by BP (British Petroleum). Investments from other countries increased 5 percent, mostly because of increasing investments from China. Different from the year 2013, the 2014 share of portfolio and investments of other types were important in funding the deficit.

Portfolio investments of 2014 created 247 million US Dollars, which is more than the index of previous year at 289 million US Dollars (in 2013, 43 million outflow of portfolio investments was fixed). In the growth of portfolio investments, the main share belonged to foreign capital attracted by the banking sector.

Funding the deficit of current account was relatively increased compared with the year 2013. In 2014, net inflow of other investments created 218 million US Dollars. Growth of other investments was mostly due to loans attracted by the governmental sector. In 2014, Government of Georgia attracted 568.1 million US Dollars in the form of loans, 118 million US Dollars of which was loans from the international monetary fund. Herewith, in 2014 the Government covered debt of the International monetary Fund in the amount of 184.0 million US Dollars.

Outcomes in the tax balance of the 1st quarter of 2015 were not characterized by great changes.

In the fourth quarter of 2014, the deficit of the current account in GDP made 13.8, which is 4.3 interest points higher than the previous year index. In absolute image deficit of current account in the fourth quarter of 2014 made 626.7 million US Dollars, which is more than the index of previous year at 192 million US Dollars. According to the preliminary assessment, the ratio of the deficit of current account in the first quarter of 2015 with GDP was 14.9% - 4.9 more percentage points than the previous year index.

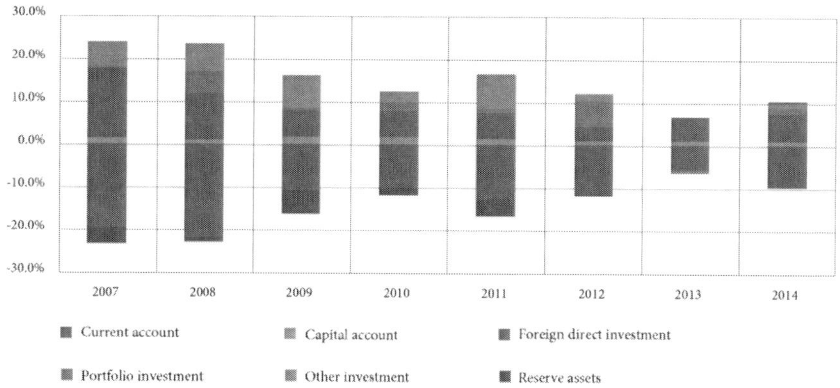

Source: National bank of Georgia.

Chart 6. Sources of funding of the deficit of current account.

Similar to the previous periods, in the first quarter of 2015 the deficit of trading goods continued deepening, which was mostly due to the worsening deficit of current account. According to preliminary data, in the first quarter of 2015, transfers (secondary incomes) were reduced as well as incomes received from trading with services.

Worsening of foreign demand in the first quarter of 2015 influenced negatively upon Georgian exports. During this period, export of goods registered was reduced 28% per annum. Exports were reduced in 194.5 million US Dollars.

Changes in exports were unequal according to the regions; in the first quarter of 2015, exports increased 19.2% to the European Union, and exports were reduced in 55.3% in CIS states. Exports were slightly reduced to other countries (-2.8%). Among CIS states, exports were sharply reduced in Azerbaijan (-56%), Armenia (-55%), Russia (-60%), Ukraine (-75%) and Kazakhstan (-59%). In other states reduction of export was mostly due to reduction of exports to Turkey (-20%) and USA (-39.3%). Exports to China increased (+144.4%), the main share of which came on re-export.

Among separate export commodities, in the first quarter of 2015 exports of wine (-67%), other alcoholic spirits (-59%), mineral waters (-34%) and fertilizers (-47%) were sharply decreased per annum. Re-export of vehicles was sharply reduced as well (-62%). Reduction of exports was particularly alleviated with the growth of export of nuts (+139%), and medical means (+84%). Re-export of copper concentrates also increased (+19%).

Table 2. Tax balance in 2010-2014 (million US Dollars)

Name	2010	2011	2012	2013	2014
Current account	-1,193	-1,841	-1,855	-930	-1,611
Commodity	-2,590	-3,494	-4,216	-3,493	-4,225
Service	513	747	1,101	1,405	1,341
Incomes (net)	-215	-423	-147	-308	-158
Transfer (net)	1,098	1,329	1,408	1,466	1,432
Capital account	206	153	134	134	115
Financial account	1,019	1,672	1,744	824	1,546
Direct investments (net)	679	902	614	829	1,077
Including direct investments in Georgia	814	1,048	911	949	1,279
Portfolio investment (net)	250	133	848	-37	210
Financial derivatives (net)	1	5	5	-2	8
Other investments (net)	297	1,205	314	-12	218
Including state sector	336	278	398	490	355
Reserve assets	-208	-572	-38	45	33
Net errors and gaps	-33	15	-23	-28	-50
Important ratio					
Reserve assets in the months of import of future year (month)	3,4	3,7	3,7	3,4	3,7
Export/Import (goods and services)	-66,2%	-65,7%	-66,0%	-77,5%	-71,1%
Current account/GDP (interest)	-10,2%	-12,7%	-11,7%	-5,8%	-9,7%
Direct investments/GDP (interest)	5,8%	6,2%	3,9%	5,1%	6,5%
Tourist incomes/GDP (interest)	5,7%	6,6%	8,9%	10,7%	10,8%
Cash transfers/GDP (interest)	9,0%	8,8%	8,4%	9,2%	8,7%

Source: National Bank of Georgia.

In the first quarter of 2015, the main reason for reduction of export was the Russia-Ukrainian conflict, as well as slowing economic growth of other countries of the region and sharp devaluation of currencies, which was accompanied by tightened regulations on the import of cars. Subject to the fact that during the last period, particular economic stabilization was noted in the Region, we may say that the rate of reduction of exports reached its maximum and on the basis of existing information, future reduction of exports is not expected. It is noteworthy that since April of 2015 (due to market effects) the rate of reduction of re-exported cars was reduced.

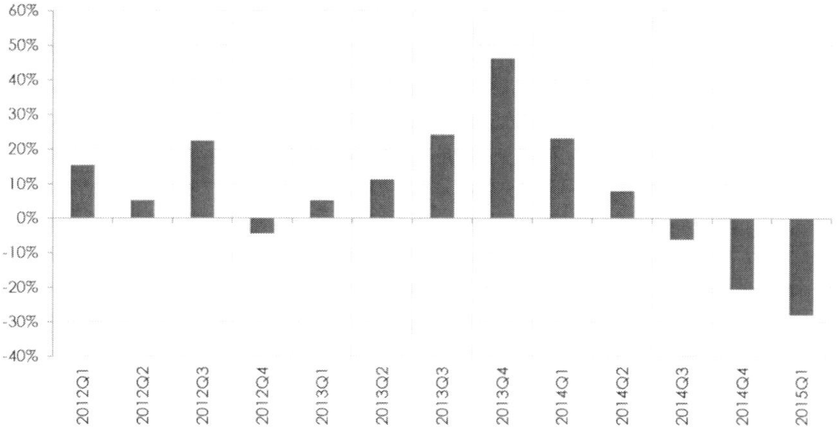

Source: Geostat.

Chart 7. Growth of export of registered goods per annum.

Imports of goods registered in the first quarter of 2015 were reduced 3.4% per annum. This was mostly due to a 33% reduction of imported oil products, which was provoked by the reduction of global prices on energy carriers. A slight reduction in the import of electric devices, of different types, was also significant. Notwithstanding an annual 3% reduction in the first quarter of 2015, the largest imported goods were still passenger cars. In the background of weak local demand and a reduction in re-exports, that import will be reduced faster in the following periods.

According to separate commodity groups, analysis of imports show that in the first quarter of 2015 reduction of import was mostly related to goods of commodity type (-11%). Import of goods of investment type was also reduced (-3%), while import of goods of intermediary type was increased by 7%.

Crisis developing in the Region negatively reflected cash transfers. In the first quarter of 2015 cash transfers were reduced 22.8% and made 250 million US Dollars. Reduction was mostly provoked by reduction of transfers from Russia 43.7%; the transfers were also reduced from Greece (-17.9%) and Italy (-9.5%), 47.1% reduction was identified in cash transfers from the Ukraine as well. Total transfers from CIS states were reduced 41.1% and from European Union – 11.3%. In the first quarter of 2015, cash transfers were increased from the USA and Turkey, respectively 27.7% and 30.5%.

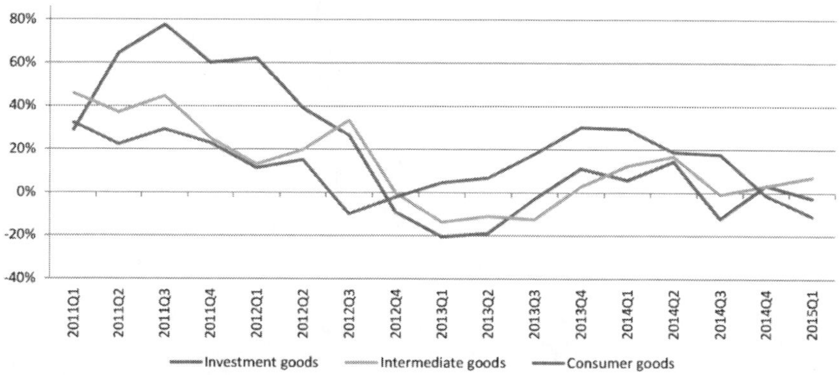

Source: Geostat and National Bank of Georgia.

Chart 8. Growth rate of import per commodity groups per annum.

In the first quarter of 2015, the amount of visitors entering Georgia was reduced 2.4% per annum. During this period, reduction of the amount of visitors was provoked by reduction of the amount of visitors from Turkey (-9.8%), Ukraine (-12.5%) and Russia (-4.5%).

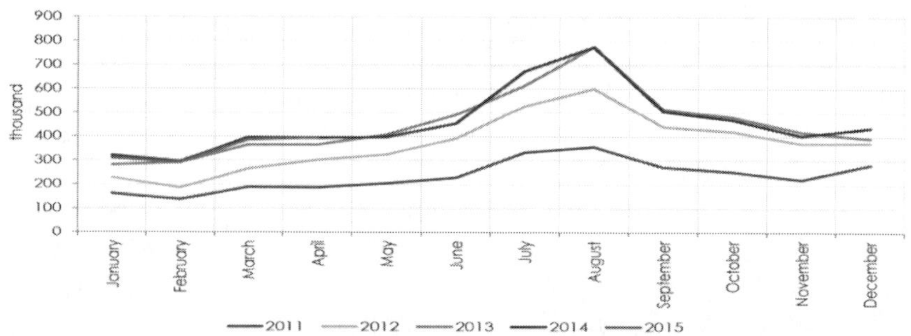

Source: Geostat.

Chart 9. Amount of visitors entering the country per months.

As for the sources of funding deficit of current accounts, in the fourth quarter of 2014, the deficit will be funded mostly with other investments and direct foreign investments. Inflow of other investments in the fourth quarter of 2014 was 326.7 million US Dollars, which is more than the index of the previous year at 181.2 million US dollars. The main source of growth of other investments was taking long-term debt by the government. Important share in the funding deficit belonged to direct foreign investments as well. Direct foreign investments in Georgia were increased in 49.2% in the fourth quarter of 2014 and made 349.2 million US Dollars.

Therefore, let us formulate reasons for reduction of foreign incomes.

Circumstances developed in 2014 that gave rise to challenges to the Georgian economy at a global and regional level, which is quite vulnerable to foreign shocks as it is a small and open economy. These circumstances gave rise to the background of strong foreign shock, having a negative impact on the economy causing a sharp reduction of inflows of foreign incomes. Reasons giving rise to the said events are:

- In 2014 and first quarter of 2015, parallel to the positive economic trends and expectations in the USA, the US Dollar started appreciation. This was accompanied with publication of decisions made on leaving the policy of quantitative alleviation started in 2008 by the Federal Reserve System, which strengthened positions of US dollars. Consequently, most of the monetary units of the world appeared in front of important devaluation.
- In January 2015, the Central Bank of Europe starting to apply monetary policy of quantitative alleviation. Quantitative alleviation program of the Central European Bank, expressed in active purchasing of the sovereign bonds, will be continued till September of 2016. This created additional pressure in devaluation of the Euro.
- At a regional level, geopolitical risks were eliminated in the first part of the year, further realization of which had negative impact over economic trends of trading partner countries. Russian-Ukrainian conflict and relative economic sanctions determined against Russia had a sharp negative effect on their economies. It is also noteworthy that crisis in Russia has a contagious effect over other countries of the Region, including important trading partners of Georgia – Armenia and Azerbaijan.
- Sharp reduction of oil prices was detected at international markets last year, which also had a negative impact on the economic perspectives of Russia and Azerbaijan.

Influence of the said factors created a sharp reduction of export of goods and services, particularly income from the tourist industry. Reduction was also fixed in cases of monetary transfer, being an important source of income of Georgian citizens.

Reduction of incomes from exports started after August of 20174 and reached maximal limit (35%) in November. During the following months, rates of reduction of export slowed and it fluctuates within the bounds of 20-30%.

The largest bit in reduction of incomes made from Georgian exports was made by a sharp reduction of exports in Azerbaijan, Armenia, Ukraine and Russia.

Sales in Azerbaijan were characterized with reduction trends from April 2014. The reason for this was determining regulations on the import of cars by Azerbaijan. This was accompanied with reduction of prices on oil at the international markets, which was negatively reflected on import opportunities of Azerbaijan. Consequently, re-export of cars to Azerbaijan for the end of the first quarter of 2015 was reduced about 70%, and reduction of entire export was 56%. Outcome of reduction of re-export of cars is reduction of exports to Armenia. According to the data of the first quarter of the year 2015, re-export of passenger cars and trucks to Armenia is reduced 80% per annum, and reduction of the entire export equals 55%. As we have noted above, reduction of exports to Ukraine is also important. The military conflict, which took place in the eastern industrial part of the Country, had a hard impact on the Ukrainian economy. Entire issue was reduced 6.8% in 2044m and local currency was significantly depreciated with all main trading partners. Consequently, exports during 2014 in Ukraine were rapidly reduced. Trends of reduction were fixed in almost every export product. Consequently, the rate of reduction during the year reached 30%. Another sharp reduction was fixed in the first three months of 2015, when exports to Ukraine were reduced 70 percent on average. According to the data of March of 2015, annual reduction of exports during first quarter was 60% with some reduction of exports of Georgia.

Therefore, economic and political circumstances developed in the Region were reflected completely on the export of Georgia. Incomes received from exports to the main export markets, is in fact reduced to the historical minimum and further reduction is not expected.

Reduction of cash transfers started from October 2014, though during summer months, growth was only 0.5 percent at average. From November-December important reduction was fixed. During the first quarter of 2015, sums entering the country by means of cash transfers were 22% on average.

As for the direction to the Europe, no reduction was fixed until autumn of 2014; though during following periods, cash transfers from such countries as Greece, Italy and Spain, making the largest share in this segment, started reduction and this trend continued in 2015. Though, at the background of total reduction it is noteworthy that the dynamic of cash transfers from the USA and Turkey were characterized with important rates.

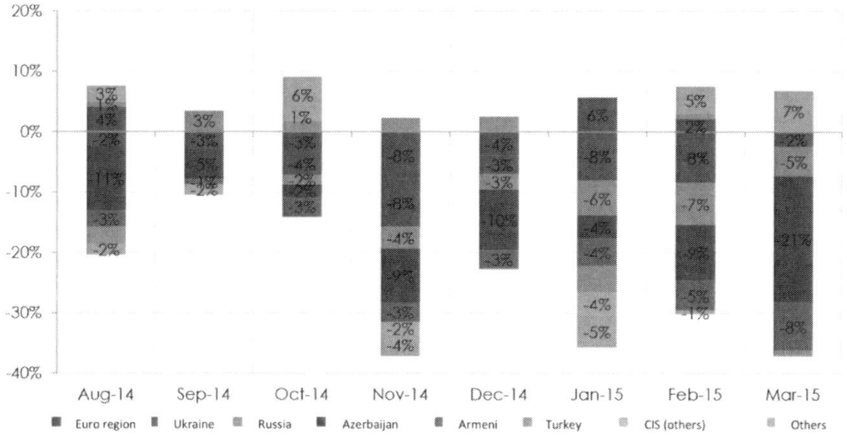

Source: National Bank of Georgia.

Chart 10. Share of export markets in the growth of export[1].

The main reason for reduction was a sharp decrease in the transfers from the largest source of cash transfers– Russia. Share of Russia, which was more than 50% during the years, reduced to 35%. In 2014, transfers from Russia were gradually decreased. Entered sums were less than 11.5% per annum compared to the previous year. At the end of the year 2014 and beginning of 2015, reduction rates overcame 40%, share of which in total index of reduction of cash transfers was more than 20%. At the same time, transfers from Ukraine were being reduced. Therewith, in such case rates of reduction were higher. The sums transfers from Ukraine in 2014 were reduced 32%. The last months of the year are the most significant, when reduction reached 60%. From the beginning of 2015, reduction of cash transfers slowed and the rate of reduction was within 45%.

[1] According to this regulation, Azerbaijan determined restriction on the import of cars manufactured before the year 2005.

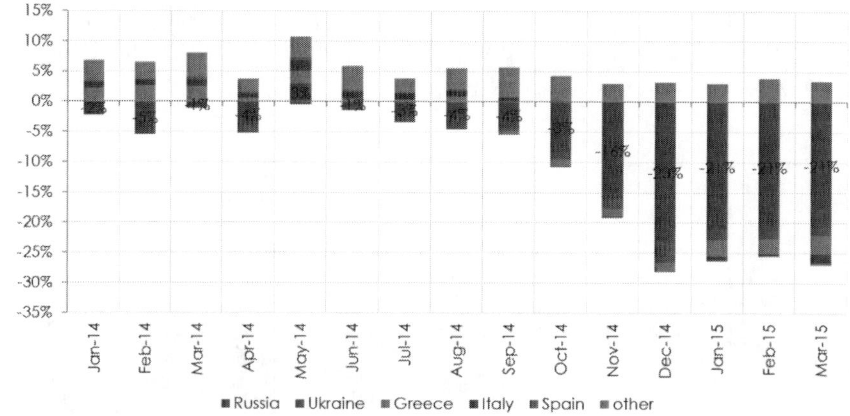

Source: Geostat.

Chart 11. Share of countries in annual growth of cash transfers.

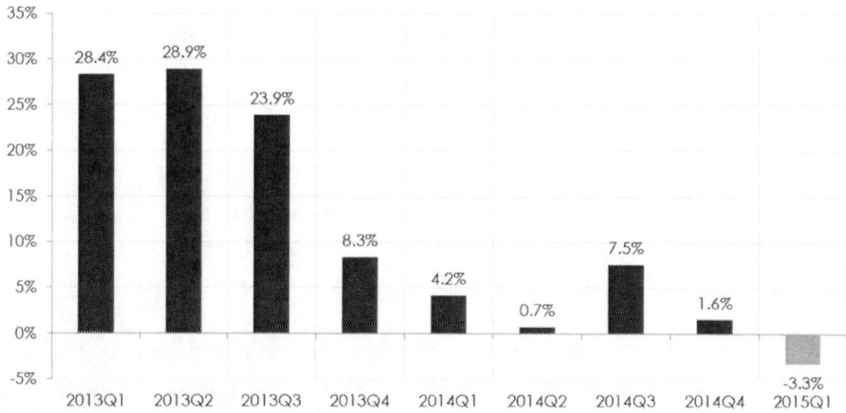

Source: National Bank of Georgia.

Chart 12. Growth rate of tourist inflows per annum.

Trends existed in the region also formed the main reasons for reduction of tourist incomes, being developed dynamically during the last several years. In the second part of 2013, the rate of growth decreased significantly. In 2014, incomes received from tourism export compared with previous years increased only 4%, which is a very low index based on the trend of precious periods. As for the first quarter of the year 2015, subject to the preliminary evaluation, it is expected to have reduction in tourist inflows of about 3.3% in the economy.

Therefore, as seen in the given analysis, the influence of negative foreign shocks was completely reflected on the economy of Georgia through different channels. Unless we receive additional shocks, further reduction of incomes is not expected.

Thus, let us summarize whether flows of US Dollars lead to further devaluation of Lari.

Current account. In the 1st quarter of 2015, deficit of current account of the tax balance was 464 million 752 thousand Georgian Laris, which is more than GDP of the first quarter by 14%. Compared to the first quarter of last year, the deficit of current account was worsened in 27%.

Foreign trade – pressure on Georgian Lari was removed. The situation became worse mostly with the increased deficits of foreign trades. Namely, if during the first quarter of last year, the deficit of foreign trade was 849 million US Dollars (i.e., import was 1.83 billion US Dollars, and export was 982 million US Dollars), in the first quarter of the current year the deficit increased to 970 million US Dollars, in 121 million US Dollars. Experts and international organizations regarded the economic problems existing in main trading partner countries to be the main reason for the reduction of exports; relatively export was decreased by 26%. Imports are reduced as well by 8%, which is an important factor for avoidance of further devaluation of Georgian Lari.

Service domain – less than 12 million US dollars from the rendered service. In the first quarter of 2015, incomes from services domain made 214 million US Dollars, playing an important role in neutralization of negative trading balance. Though, it should be noted that incomes made from the service sector, compared with last year, were reduced 5.4%.

Income from the transport domain is reduced as well, though 16% growth is fixed in the incomes of the railway sector.

There is a 3.9% reduction in incomes made through tourism. If in the first quarter of last year incomes made from tourism were more than 250 million US Dollars, this year 241 million US Dollars were made.

Transfers are reduced 7% - from 687 million US Dollars to 329 million US Dollars.

Capital and financial reporting. The second part of the tax balance is capital and financial reporting, which is an important source of funding the deficit of current account. Outflow of the mass of foreign currency, formed by means of high import and low export, is covered with other resources of direct investments and financial reporting.

Capital and financial reporting in the first quarter of the year 2015, compared to the same period of last year, improved 18% and increased from 387 million US Dollars to 458 million US Dollars.

Reduction is detected from the point of direct foreign investments. The negative balance of portfolio investments was 38.4 million US dollars. The balance of other investments in the first quarter of 2015 was 175.4 million US Dollars.

Relatively, capital and financial reporting covered the deficit of current account almost completely.

Table 3. Data of the 1st quarter of 2014 and 1st quarter of the year 2015 of tax balance

	2014, Quarter I	2015, Quarter I	Outcome
Current account	-365,874.2	-464,752.7	Worsened
a. Commodity	-849,686.9	-970,668,2	Worsened
b. Service	226,779.3	214,664.8	Worsened
c. Income	-97,536.3	-38,686,4	Improved
d. Current transfers	354,569.7	329,937.1	Worsened
Capital and financial reporting	387,819.5	458,671.3	Improved
Capital reporting	12,265.2	17,028.5	Improved
Financial reporting	375,554.3	441,642.8	Improved
a. Direct investments	232,190.9	117,485.6	Worsened
b. Portfolio investments	-16,622.1	-38,388.8	Worsened
c. Financial derivatives	2,953.8	2,371.9	Worsened
d. Other investments	-71,809.4	175,394.2	Improved
e. Reserve assets	228,841.0	184,779.9	Worsened
Net errors and gaps	-21,945.3	6,081.4	Improved
Special funding – total	17,433.2	46,245.9	Improved

Source: Data of National Bank of Georgia.

Chapter 3

DOES FOREIGN DEBT INFLUENCE THE EXCHANGE RATE OF GEORGIAN LARI?

According to some economists, one of the factors conditioning the drop in the exchange rate of Georgian Lari is changing the situation regarding the entire foreign debt of Georgia. We take one billion and a half Georgian Laris almost annually. Now we do not take debt on this scale and, of course, inflow of currency is reduced in this regard.

This is a positive factor from the point that the debt is not increased in the country more than the economy, i.e., we are not debt-depended. Though earlier, the debt was being increased more rapidly than the economy (this leads to a situation like Greece).

To be more precise, since obtaining independence in Georgia, especially in the period from 2003 through 2012, the currency deficit was funded by increasing the entire foreign debt of Georgia. For example, if the 2012 total foreign debt of Georgia was increased by 1600 billion, in 2011 by 1400 billion, then foreign debt was being increased about one billion and half per annum, by means of which deficit of currency was compensated by deficit of the US Dollar, which is the main factor of appreciation of currency.

Factor of foreign debt is too noteworthy for evaluation of the state of the economy and national debt in general. On October 23, 2008 after the Brussels Conference, international donors allocated 4.5 billion US Dollars to Georgia. It shall be noted that during the next 4 years, national currency greatly depended on the billion-US Dollar injection annually. If we add the growth of the volume of foreign debt to this, it appears that through the year 2013, strengthening of national currency partially depended on the foreign debt and not the real state of the economy.

The year 2013 was the first year in the history of Georgia that total foreign debt of Georgia was not increased, but reduced by 50 million US Dollars. This is a kind of a shock when you are accustomed, i.e., when you lack US Dollars, you take loans and regulate everything. This factor will be removed. In such case, of course, it is difficult to regulate the situation.

Today, the drop in the national exchange rate of the national currency is kind of returning the economy to the point where it really is. This datum shall be recognized, i.e., we shall share the state of our economy and our economic policy shall be planned from the real conditions.

Unfortunately, the stability of the Georgian Lari depends greatly upon foreign credit and grants, as the economy of the country will not attract foreign currency of the amount needed to assist the stability of Georgian Lari. For strengthening this opinion, it would be necessary to set trends of current and capital and financial reporting of tax balances of the years 2000-2014.

Our country has an economy that doesn't attract US Dollars. At the background of devaluation of Georgian Lari, they often speak about disability of the government and they bring forward an argument that during previous government, the exchange rate of Georgian Lari against US Dollars was much stronger. Though, as it is seen from the tax balance named above, reflecting economic operations between Georgia and the remaining world, i.e., reflecting foreign cash mass entering the country or leaving it, it becomes clear that during 15 years, the structure of the economy of Georgia was not changed in the way of attracting foreign currency through increasing exports or other resources. The trade balance was and remains sharply deficient, due to which, the mass of foreign currency received through investments, transfers and other resources, only neutralize, nullifying foreign currency flowing out of the country, i.e., the amount of foreign currency entering the country is the same as that leaving it.

Current capital and financial reporting shows that the mass of foreign currency is attracted by the economy excluding credits and grants. If we look at Chart 2, we will see "actor-proof tragedy," i.e., the reality that during 15 years, the mass of foreign currency attracted without credits and grants was slightly more than 100 million US Dollars. The volume of foreign currency entering the country during 15 years was more than the volume of currency flowing out the country only 8 times.

Looking through the statistics of foreign debt during last the 15 years, total foreign debt (as governmental, so - private) of Georgia was increased almost 6 times and as of September 30, 2014, it was more than 13 billion US

Dollars. State debt of the governmental sector for the same period of time was increased 3.5 times.

Today, they, especially political figures, often speak about the fact that they provide growth of reserves and stability of Georgian Lari, though they seldom speak about the phenomenon at the expense of which it was "achieved." Source of stability of reserves and Georgian Lari was not directed to the forwardness of economy, but inflow of foreign credits. As 75% of the entire foreign debt of the country in 2006-2012 was recognized, i.e., in half of the 15 years they increased 75% of foreign debt [9].

These were the credits providing formation of reserves and assistance of Georgian Laris, but since 2013, the country started refunding foreign debt in great amounts and as it is seen from the Chart 4, foreign debt practically stopped increasing. Consequently, at the background of deficit tax balance, an important source of foreign currencies in the country – foreign credits – "slipped out" of our hands, and the growth of reserves (see the Chart 5) and assistance of exchange of Georgian Lari could not be provided.

Therewith, we consider it to be purposeful to use one phenomenon announced in media, which we do not speak about today. Notwithstanding the fact that the volume of foreign debt expressed in US Dollars has almost been unchanged, the Georgian budget will have to pay more than 2.7 billion Georgian Laris for repayment of foreign debts. Why?

If in 2012, foreign debt was 6.6 billion Georgian Laris, for 2015 it has increased by 2.7 billion Georgian Laris up to 9.3 billion Georgian Laris.

Has foreign debt truly been increased?

Conclusion: foreign debt has almost not increased: if in 2012 foreign debt expressed in foreign debt was 3.997 billion US Dollars, in 2014 it was 5.027 billion US Dollars. This is mostly the "outcome" of a sharp drop in the exchange rate of Georgian Lari [10].

As we have noted above, the year 2015 in Georgia began with reduction of foreign debt.

In the first quarter of 2015, total foreign debt of Georgia compared with the same period of last year increased 1.5% or 13 billion 424 million US Dollars.

Statistics of the last 15 years of foreign debt of the country are given in the Chart below.

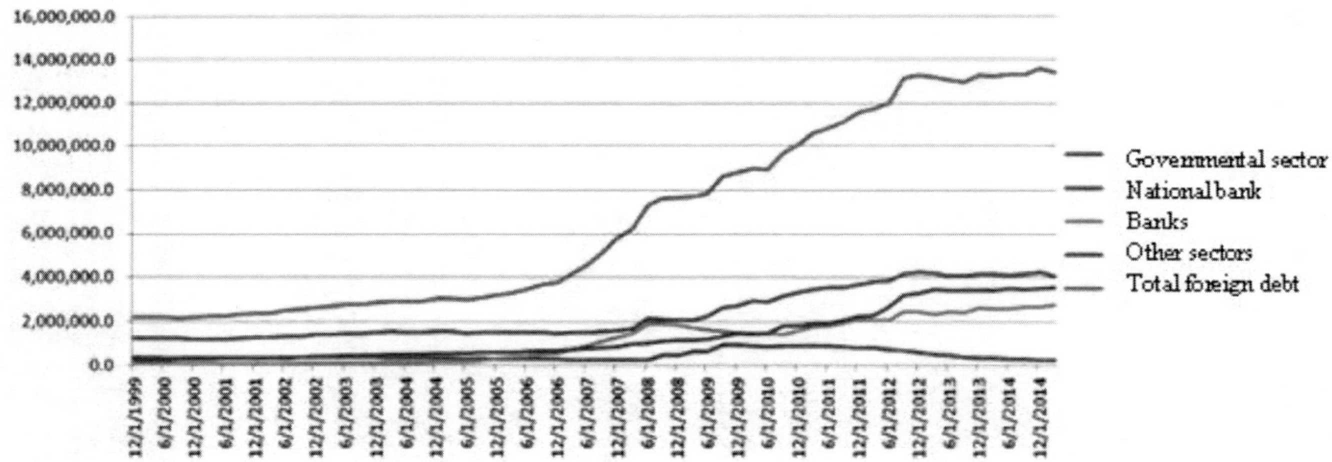

Chart 13. Statistics of the last 15 years of foreign debt of the country.

As you can see in the Chart, the rate of growth of total foreign debt of the Country was especially high in the years 2006-2012; i.e., the economy, which didn't attract foreign currency by development, used to attract its debts, making it the source for stability of Georgia Lari and increasing foreign reserves.

As you might know, statistics of total foreign debt includes foreign debt of state (governmental sector, state enterprise and national bank) and private sector (banking and other sectors).

Total foreign debt of Georgia as of March 31 of 2015, amounted to 13.4 billion US Dollars (29.9 billion Georgian Laris), 82.8 percent of GDP of the last four quarters; among this, state foreign debt was 5.1 billion US Dollars (11.5 billion Georgian Laris), or 31.7 percent of GDP, including debt of the government sector in the amount of 4.1 billion US Dollars (9.1 billion Georgian Laris; 25.1 percents of GDP), obligations of the National Bank – 232.0 million US Dollars (516.9 million Georgian Laris; 1.4 percent of GDP), and bonds of state enterprises and loans, respectively, 837.1 million US Dollars (1.9 billion Georgian Laris; 5.2 percent of GDP) and 588.1 million US Dollars (1.3 billion Georgian Laris; 3.6 percent of GDP). Foreign debt of the banking sector was 2.8 billion US Dollars (6.1 billion Georgian Laris; 17.0 percent of GDP), and foreign debt of other sectors – 3.6 billion US Dollars (7.9 billion Georgian Laris; 22 percent of GDP) and intercompany debt was 2.8 US Dollars (6.3 billion Georgian Laris, 17.3 percent of GDP). 94.2 percent of total foreign debt is denominated with foreign currency.

Foreign obligations of the government sector during the reporting period were reduced 177.0 million US Dollars (366.9 million Georgian Laris). By means of changing the exchange rate and operational changes, the debt was reduced respectively by 172.3 million US Dollars (357.2 million Georgian Laris) and 33.9 million US Dollars (70.2 million Georgian Laris). And due to the change in price it was increased 29.2 million US Dollars (60.5 million Georgian Laris).

It is noteworthy that growth of foreign debt was provided actively from 2005. Since 2013, the country moved to the active regime of repayment of foreign debt, due to which the rate of increase of foreign debt significantly dropped, almost nullified.

Investment position – the assets increased faster than obligations. International investment position reflects balances of foreign financial assets and obligations at a particular moment of time.

Net international investment position of Georgia as of March 31, 2015 was 16.8 billion US Dollars (-37.5 billion Georgian Laris), making 103.8

percent of GDP. Said index compared to the respective period of the previous year increased 338.4 million US Dollars (753.8 million Georgian Laris), and compared to the previous quarter it was reduced 417.4 million US Dollars (865.3 Million Georgian Laris).

Assets. As of March 31 of 2015, total international assets were 5.7 billion US Dollars (12.8 billion Georgian Laris). 42.7 percent belong to reserve assets; 31.6 percent by other investments; 24.6 percent from direct investments abroad; and 1.1 percent from the investments of portfolio and financial derivatives.

Obligations. As for the obligations, at the end of the first quarter total obligations were 22.6 billion US Dollars (50.3 billion Georgian Laris), being more than the index of the similar period of last year by 318.4 million US Dollars (709.3 million Georgian Laris), compared with the index of the previous quarter, it was reduced 801.3 million US Dollars (1.8 billion Georgian Lari).

As seen from the foreign statistics, at the background of entering currency flows inflow of money from particular sources was increased, as well as reduction of outflow of currency, for example, from imports. No signs of further devaluation of Georgian Lari are identified in the existing statistics. Truly, after the first quarter, no important fluctuations of Georgian Lari have taken place.

The economists recognize that present resonance around National Currency speaks for the fact that this is not inflation by devaluation. It will be inflation in case of increasing index of consumer basket [1].

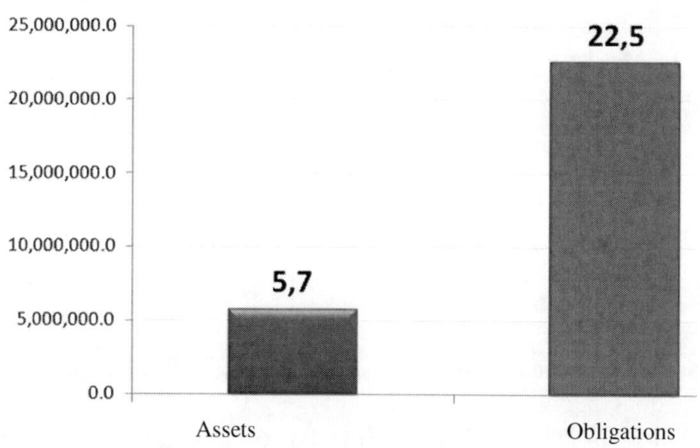

Chart 14. Investment position (billion US Dollars).

Chapter 4

WHAT ARE OUTCOMES OF GEORGIAN LARI AND WHOSE FAULT IS IT?

The main problem is inflation, as devaluation creates rising prices on imported products. There are multiple factors, because of which there is no sharp inflation risk in Georgia. First, Lari has not been devalued against the currencies of the countries where imports are coming from – European Union, Turkey, Russia; second, reduction of the price of oil stopped inflation; **third,** inflation is 1.4% today, notwithstanding the fact that it will be increased, the National Bank prognosis is 5%. Though, notwithstanding the fact that these establishments having loans in US Dollars keep increasing prices, and suppliers of natural air declared that it would increase prices on air for legal entities [1] (and it did, L.Q.).

As for Georgian Lari, if there are no levers for its solution, to appreciation Georgian Lari on particular reasonable marking. We consider such level to be 1.194/1.95 conformity. People would get used to it.

Some economists note that getting used to the process of devaluation of Georgian Lari is inadmissible. It is gruesome to think of such luxury in the country with economic and social background; it will give rise to great feelings of instability, and this will exhaust reliability of credit of the Government, leading the country into deadlock.

"Developments depend on the actions of the National Bank, namely what the steps of the National Bank of Georgia will be in connection with devaluation of Georgian Lari and if the Central Bank allows more devaluation of the National Currency.

Some economists consider the process of devaluation to be the reason for achieving the index of inflation declared by the National Bank. Georgian Lari today is depreciated and it doesn't reflect the potential of the economy of our country. Due to this, Devaluation of Georgian Lari is necessary for healthy development of the economy – not with a sharp drop within a short period of time, but with gradual weakening over a long term period.

"Development of events depends on the actions of the national Bank, when this latest declares that it has targeted inflation and it cannot reach marking of the said inflation, affecting negatively upon development of economy… Strange though it might sound, but when there were inflation indexes of 8-9%, the highest rates of product growth were identified in Georgia. And with low rates of inflation, growth of Gross Domestic Product was less detected; due to this, the National Bank must reach the inflation rate declared by it" [13].

Targeted inflation is mainly what the National Bank is working with.

Decision of monetary policy is based on the macroeconomic prognosis, according to which risks and expectations influencing upon predicted inflation by means of foreign shocks were increased. Notwithstanding appreciation of the nominal effective exchange rate of Georgian Lari, the last devaluation of the exchange rate against the US Dollar was reflected on the growth of intermediary changes related with the service of loans denominated in US Dollars.

Based on the foregoing, in the following months they expect particular growth of the inflation index. Due to the fact that foreign and domestic demand is significantly reduced, the monetary committee considers influence of the above factors over inflation will be of short-term nature and it doesn't give rise to inflation risks for the medium-term period. Therefore, the committee of monetary policy considers maintenance of the rate of monetary policy unchanged at the given stage. Together with improvement of foreign and domestic economic situation, the process of leaving alleviated monetary policy will be implemented gradually.

Notwithstanding the fact that national currency has been significantly devaluated, the National Bank is not going to limit loans of refinancing. Besides this, it shall be noted that to achieve targeted inflation, the National Bank of Georgia increased the volume of refinancing loans up to the recorded – 900 million Georgian Laris. If we add to this the fact that interest rates of these loans have not been increased, it is doubtless that appreciation of Georgian Lari will not be allowed before achievement of targeted inflation by the National Bank [14].

With the background of reciprocal claims, after ordinary users, business appeared to be in a difficult situation: reduced sales, expensive credits and imports, increased expenditures and lease payments.

Strengthening monetary policy by the National Bank will slow the increase in prices, though it has a side effect as well:

This change, which took place recently, will have a direct influence upon the persons who have taken loans in Georgian Laris. Their exchange rate will become more expensive. The banks have in the agreement that they will raise the interest rate, if the rate of refinancing becomes higher. Making loans expensive is not necessary in accordance with the exchange rate of the National Bank. This is subject to decision by the banks. Finally, this is not good. This means the policy of expensive money could mean less money will enter into the economy" [15].

The hardest situation was formed with the legal entities and individuals receiving income in Georgian Laris, and loans in US Dollars. As in most developing countries, there is high level of dollarization in Georgia. 60% of bank loans are issued in US Dollars. Many companies have loans in US Dollars, and 80% of installments and the retail market are issued in US Dollars. These persons today will pay more; 15-20% in National Currency.

Some economists gave very strict assessment to the National Bank:

- "National Bank holds every lever to maintain the rate it considers to be necessary." Counter-repost: - did emission take place with participation of the National Bank – budget was filled with this money in December, which continued in January and it resulted in what we have today;
- The President of the National Bank recognized that it was acting under the influence of the Government – he said that it doesn't welcome funding of the budget and this will not be continued in the way as it happened last year – it means that interference took place, as National Bank is prohibited by law to fund the budget.

These figures may not be posted anywhere, though it is evident that mass cash has entered the economy;

- When depth of devaluation of Georgian Lari reached 20% and it formed "nutritious" grounds for currency speculations, National Bank of Georgia used interventions most intensively during this period; upon elimination of signs of currency speculation and receiving universal nature of panics, intensive investment activities became necessary; at the same time more effective and consistent communication with the society [M. Kakulia];

- "When you see that there is access of Georgian Lari, there is demand on US Dollar and at the same time it increases crediting of commercial banks from 350 million to 700 million, thus placing huge mass into circulation…when stability of the exchange rate of Georgian Lari is of serious danger and truly destructive process is provided…" This is what the National Bank of Georgia exists for, to insure the country from the influence of foreign factors. Due to this, it is the National Bank that assumes huge responsibility for the said situation" [16];
- "…This is why these bodies are created to minimize negative processes inside the county and the processes taking place outside the country, affecting us. After identification of the exchange rate of Georgian Lari, on November 3 of 2014 this process was started, what does it speak about? This means that conformity of Georgian Lari and US Dollars was violated at the market and at the same time, you increase Georgian Lari in circulation instead of its reduction…what does it mean?

At this time, the National Bank undertakes obligation to make money a bit more expensive and to have small amount of Georgian Laris within possible bounds" [2].

For stabilization of the exchange rate of Georgian Lari, except international currency reserves, the National Bank has other means of intervention, which influence upon exchange rate of Georgian Lari, namely, the National Bank has the opportunity to regulate the mass of Georgian Lari in the economy with the rate of refinancing.

Though, the National Bank used this opportunity incorrectly during the last months – on one hand, it provided the market with the mass of US Dollars, and thus reduced international currency reserves and, on the other hand, by means of the mechanism of the rate of refinancing also increased delivery of the mass of Georgian Lari.

Finally, the first intervention was neutralized at the expense of another and it lost positive effect, which should be achieved by means of delivering mass of US Dollars" [17].

National Bank implements interventions, as in Georgian Laris, so – in US Dollars. National Bank feels when and what sums are required (this is what they receive remuneration for!). This is the matter of pure competence and professionalism. At the beginning of the fluctuation of the exchange rate, it shall be stopped and decreased. Generally, change in the rate is a normal phenomenon, though this change shall not be abrupt and in direction of one trend [18].

From the negative factor, almost every expert recognizes the fact that the problem of cash transfers through rapid cash transfers appeared during the last months. Notwithstanding the fact that during last months of last year compared with the similar months of 2013, were reduced from abroad, in fact, it was insignificantly reduced during the year.

In 2014, through the channels of fast transfers 1.441 billion US Dollars were transferred, and 1477 billion were transferred in 2013. These two indexes are higher than the data of 2012 (1.334 billion) and 2011 (1.268).

As we can see, here we do not speak about reduction, but interruption in the trend of growth arising during the last years!

Avoidance of greater reduction is conditioned with the fact that, different from the Middle East or Armenia, where most transfers are provided by Russia - it is diversified in Georgia. Half of transfers come from Russia, but the other half is implemented by up to twenty countries of the world; even growth is noted from some of them.

Conclusion: with great probability, the volume of money transferred from Russia will be reduced; the amount of total transfers shall not be lower than the index of 2013.

Implementation of intervention with the principle the more US Dollars are purchased by the National Bank, the same amount shall be sold by it in case pressure over the rate of Georgian Lari *is not correct*. This depends on the fact, under what conditions recovery of foreign currency takes place and later, under what conditions are they used in course of regulation of the exchange rate. 555 million US Dollars were recovered in terms, when US Dollars flowed into Georgian economy relatively more intensive.

During the period (I mean the first three quarters of 2013) there was an excess amount of US Dollars at the interbank market and if the National Bank of Georgia would not take this excess amount of US Dollars from circulation, Georgian Lari would be unjustifiably appreciated, which would influence badly upon competition ability of the country economy."

And the most remarkable is: when there is a global trend of increasing the exchange rate of US Dollars in the world and the currency of every main trading partner of Georgia is fallen against US Dollar, Georgian Lari cannot be left in the same state, as it was before its start.

Under the condition of floating rates, they mostly used interventions of important volume when there are short-term competitive fluctuations at the market, for neutralization of temporary misbalance, the National Bank purchases or sells US Dollars [17].

Therewith, totality of internal and external factors appeared economic for the state of the country under hard situations.

It was a mistake when they started speaking about cheap money and free loans. Another mistake was that they tried to fulfill this promise and loaded the budget with multiple obligations, which it should not have. This policy reduced the business environment; many functions were distributed from the private sectors to the state sector; bureaucracy and its costs were increased; investments were sharply reduced subject to the policy that for foreigners private ownership of land should be reduced; briefly saying, the problems originated from the budget out of the blue.

They made a mistake from the point of monetary system – the National Bank could not understand what had happened in a timely manner, and devaluation reached quite a high marking. In fact, their decisions are quite limited: nonmarket, nonindustrial, not oriented towards widening of economy, and using new opportunities (this is what is included in the functions of the National Bank – L.Q.).

Chapter 5

How Fiscal Policy Influenced Changes in the Rates of Georgian Lari

There are two principle regulators of the economy in Georgia – National Bank and Government (though we do not welcome such sharp segregation. L.Q.). As for the monetary-credit policy – prerogative of the National Bank, and provision of monetary flows, of course, is part of the economic policy of the government.

Executive government shall attract and master first tranches of grants and credits foreseen in the budget of year 2015 in maximal extent. It has been mentioned that the Country would appeal to the Monetary Fund for assistance again and invest funds into the infrastructure projects. I consider it to be incorrect, as, in the first place, we have already allocated budgetary funds of 2015 with infrastructure projects and it is too early to speak about allocation of excess planned funds in the first part of the year. In the first place, we consider it necessary to master already allocated funds and the end of the year will show the issues of allocation-non-allocation of the funds for the said purpose.

It is noteworthy that the Monetary Fund will never allocate funds for infrastructure projects. The purpose of the Monetary Fund is granting credit for stability of Georgian Lari, filling monetary reserves and systemic assistance to the budgetary process. Achievement of true positive fiscal balance remains a problem for every government of post-Soviet Georgia. True fiscal balance is not positive while budgetary incomes, excluding privatization incomes, are more than budgetary costs. After the Rose Revolution, the Georgian government was able to maintain a general positive fiscal balance for only for three years, and at the expense of incomes made from privatization. Today potential of privatization of the assets owned by the state is reduced more than it was earlier. Today, in case of negative shock on the economy, it will be very difficult for the Government to maintain positive fiscal balance without assuming debt.

In 2010, budgetary deficit made 1.38 billion Georgian Laris (6.3 of GDP), and the deficit of consolidated budget equaled to 1.41 billion Georgian Laris (6.8% of GDP). Subject to the preliminary data of 2011, this correlation was reduced to 3.7%, while the budgetary deficit was not more than 878.6 billion Georgian Laris. As it is seen from Chart 15, the largest budgetary deficit, expressed in the GDP share (9.3%) in 2009 was due to the expansive economic policy of the crisis period. For provision of macroeconomic stability, fiscal consolidation is of the greatest importance, reducing the budgetary deficit to the bearable level.

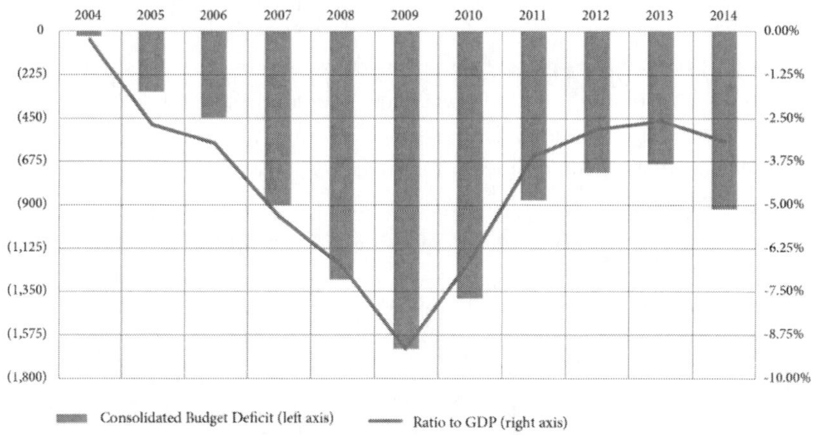

Source: National Bank of Georgia.

Chart 15. Deficit of Consolidated Budget (Million Georgian Laris) and correlation with GDP.

An important source of forming domestic demand is the fiscal sector. Deficit of the budget of 2014 made 3.2 percent, which is less by 0.6 percentage points than the planned index (see the Chart 15). Compared with 2013, the deficit increased 0.6 percentage points. In 2014, expenses of consolidated budget increased by 884 million Georgian Laris (11 percent) compared with the previous year. Cost overruns mostly touched upon current expenditures (975 million Georgian Laris), and capital inputs and net crediting were reduced 91 million Georgian Laris.

Achievement of fiscal consolidation is of the greatest importance today, as budget expenditures are being increased at an extremely quick rate. Budget expenditures per capita in Georgia have significantly overcome the rate of economic growth in general.

When state expenses reach a particular level of GDP, their profit margin is necessarily reduced. Another dangerous outcome of uncontrolled growth of the state sector is accumulation of the debt, which is a natural outcome of undesired growth of state expenditures in the GDP.

Today, levels of the state debt are much less than the level of 60% of GDP, determined by the act of economic independence. It would be a serious challenge to maintain the level of debt within manageable bounds, if the above trend continues. Consideration of absolute values of domestic and foreign debts of the country will not give much. Accepted practice for their real evaluation is their representation in the form of correlations of several indicators of debt. This is the percentage share of export and budgetary incomes. This is where the real danger of Lari is identified. In case of correlation with GDP, when debt makes an important share of GDP and the rate of growth of this debt is much more than GDP growth, recession in the economy will take place even if correlation of the debt with GDP is stabilized. As for the conformity of debt and export, this shows that total debt is being increased much faster than the main source of foreign income of the country, which speaks of the fact that the country may face problems in performance of credit obligations in the future. Herewith, correlation of debt with incomes, which is main source of domestic income of the country, shows that the budget may have problems in serving this domestic debt. In case of such negative scenario, foreign creditors are the way out, as 75% of the debt is foreign debt. In such case, the debt may be rapidly increased and damage the perspective of economic growth.

Subject to the above opinion, we consider it necessary to note the reasons for three times devaluation of Georgian Lari in one and the same consecutive period. During two years the current changes in economic policy are found, in the first place, we shall emphasize the fact that transformation of the economy oriented towards market into the socially oriented has taken place.

Concentrated expression of this is the budget. This is of an absolutely different nature. Different, so-called incentive expenditures were increased: subsidies, business programs, funding plowing and sowing in agriculture, and even crop insurance (this should be done by the insurance companies!). On the other hand, Universal Health Insurance, free books, widening the circle of beneficiaries for social allowances, as well as permanent growth of the state machine, as at the local level, in central ranges, recovering multiple regulatory norms; moreover, promoting exports, issuing export warranties, shall not take place at the expense of budget. Does it mean that those who fail in exports be funded by the budget? Another unpleasant fact – subsidies were provided to agriculture for the Russian market, and hundreds of millions of Georgian Laris. It appeared that they involved restrictions for some goods, and others are unable to enter Russia, due to the crisis.

There are much more accusations on the considered problem by the Center of Analysis and Prognosis of Tbilisi State University:

- At the initial stage of devaluation of the exchange rate of Georgian Lari, the Ministry of Finance has not implemented sharp expenditure policy, reflected in the growth of the mass of Georgian Lari.
- Obligations undertaken by the Government regarding return of untaxed minimum was directly reflected on the growth of the mass of Georgian Lari in the Georgian economy.
- In December of 2014, compared with November, the Ministry of Finance, for fixing high rate of budget execution, implemented a sharp expenditure policy, which increased mass of Georgian Lari in the economy. TSU Center of Analysis and Prognosis considers it the job of the Ministry of Finance of Georgia to look through monetary policy, as high demand on national currency by it gives impulse to the National Bank to provide commercial banks with additional mass of Georgian Lari, which, in its turn, promotes devaluation of Georgian currency [17].

Thus, in summarizing the above issues of devaluation of the Georgian monetary unit, let me refer to the conclusions of the International Monetary Fund and emphasize again that the International Monetary Fund explains phenomenon related with exchange rate of Georgian Lari with external factors: "the situation, which took place in connection with the exchange rate of Lari in the country, depends entirely upon external factors and is conditioned with external factors. For example, when currency is appreciated or devaluated in Great Britain, in such case, the Central Bank doesn't implement any interventions. The question, why was the Georgian Lari devalued several times and then appreciated during the last days? This is the factor characterizing a floating exchange rate. Consequently, it is not purposeful to make a prognosis, or take any particular measure, as it is very difficult to make determination and prognosis under the conditions of floating mode," - says Mark Griffiths.

According to his definition, the floating rate in its essence means that Georgian Lari will be appreciated and sometimes devalued in order to master and balance external factors, risks and fluctuations. "Consequently, the rate will absorb these risks and external factors. It was truly a great shock, but this is how markets react on the exchange rate. Europe and multiple other countries have suffered the same shock," – says Mark Griffiths [19].

Chapter 6

What Shall We Do to Save Georgian Lari and the Georgian Economy?!

Growth of Real Sector of Economy – Principle Means for Appreciation of Georgian Lari

We consider accelerated development of the real sector of the economy (industry, agriculture, and fields of processing industry) to be extremely necessary.

To justify our offer, I will come up with the argument: the fall of monetary units, of even such a hyper power as China, is explained by retardation of economic growth. Its economy suffers stagnation for several months.

Sharp weakening of all financial markets of the country with an economy second in size and national currency – the Yuan was provoked by weak macroeconomic indexes coming from China, such as retardation of the rate of increasing Gross Domestic Product, increasing consumer prices, a sharply reduced index of export-import, etc. Chinese analysts themselves explained the collapse of the market with economic growth of the Country. After 2009, forward economics of the Country was sharply slowed. Consequently, annual profits of companies decreased as well. At the same time, they didn't refuse the influence of so-called external factors in China, particularly, influence upon the fall in prices on raw materials worldwide, except inadequate indexes of oil production, and influence of cheapening oil was provided together with an 8% fall in the prices of shares of China. According to the Analysts, the stock exchange of China doesn't remember such outcome of the one-day fall during 8 years.

Funny though it might sound, no quarreling between the government and Central Bank of the Country took place in order to find out "who was guilty," but in the beginning of the year, the Central Bank of China accepted the decision on reducing interest rates twice in the beginning of the year. Peoples' Bank of China decreased interest rates to the record marking. In the case of commercial banks, in the course of using one-year credit, the percentage rate was reduced 25 percent and its index is fluctuating from 2.5% to 5.35%.

His decision was planned by the Central Bank of China for promoting credit, which is a forward step for simulation of economy. Such steps were not new from the side of the Central Bank of China. In the beginning of 2015, the main bank made a decision on reducing obligatory reserves for the commercial banks for promoting credits in the economy and banks (I write this for the National Bank. The author's remark). This means that in the future, the banks will release money for issuance of different credits. Moreover, it shall be noted that China has changed economic priorities of the country and made decisions on reviewing expenditures during the last period.

I can freely refer to the quote of the Academician Avtandil Silagadze, the essence of which I share and approve entirely: "application of the Government made in connection with the privatization of state property during the last period may be considered to be one of the mechanisms of monetary stability. On the other hand, for the purpose of assisting foreign investments we shall review legislation, in order to have stimulating mechanisms in maximal extent. The work shall be guided actively in direction to the development of tourism.

Production, industry, and agriculture shall be developed. For this, we shall use local resource in maximal extent, which we have of quite great amount. As for the new state foreign debt, this step, may be made, though this money shall be used purposefully, particularly for the purpose of national production and it will be effective only in such case. Previous government assumed huge debt during last 4-5 years – billions of US Dollars, but they didn't use it for development of economy. Every state takes assumed debt, but they try to use it for making profit.

Georgia holds great reserve for rising state foreign debt. Share of foreign debt is purposeful to be up to 60% of Gross Domestic Product. Today share of foreign debt with GDP is maximum 40%.

Except for infrastructure, loans shall be used for real production. During the years, we were taking billions of loans and never used it in the real sector, where real wealth is made, and where there are great reserves of employment.

Consequently, I do not support increasing such loans and its expenditures, except for infrastructural projects. The Monetary Fund didn't tell us categorically to increase taxes and not to take loans. They offered several alternatives to the government. Budget optimization, of course, is possible, but I consider it unreasonable to increase taxes under existing situations.

On the contrary, entrepreneurs and businesses shall not be restricted by increasing taxes, but we shall move to greater liberalization [20].

Professor Mikheil Tokmajishvili gives a similar recommendation for the purpose of stopping devaluation and strengthening the exchange rate of Georgian Lari. He writes: "we cannot blame any bank in devaluation of Georgian Lari. Though, the merger of several banks may influence upon exchange rate, but this will be only a single step, which will not give rise to the extended outcome… The bank cannot form crisis of exchange rate. Considering this problem, we shall focus on more objective factors, such as: the current situation in economy, investments, export opportunities of the country, level of their usage and etc."

As for the National Bank, it may generally freeze exchange rates, but in such case, the economy is entirely stopped. Due to this, we shall make a choice between the following: 1. Lari shall be devalued smoothly and not sharply, but development of the economy shall be stimulated instead and 2. We shall stop the economy, observe if Georgian Lari is stable, and be happy.

Conclusion: devaluation of Georgian Lari is not among functions and interests of the National Bank: its main objective is providing the economy with funds and maintain a low index of inflation [21, 33].

Thus, let us formulate the axiom of stopping devaluation of Georgian Lari and its further appreciation: gradual growth of systemic nature of the real economy, reversible nature of the process of economic growth, warranty of stability of Georgian Lari, in the first place, is recovering the economy of the Country.

Making the Investment Climate More Attractive to Local and Foreign Investors

It will be impossible to speak about improvement of economic growth if no investment boom takes place in Georgia. Under modern conditions, activation of investment policy is the main condition for moving the Georgian economy to sustainable economic development.

Today the main lines of the state investment policy are: strengthening the support of prior directions of economic development, creation of a legal and economic environment for institutions to promote investments in the real sector of the economy.

I consider it necessary to specify that in the process of reforming the Georgian economy, they considered foreign direct investments and development of the banking system to be the driving force for the economy. It's pleasant that both drivers of the economy are operating well today.

Foreign direct investments build a clear opinion about the amount of funds invested in gross fixed capital of the country, how attractive the country is for investment, and which fields hold opportunities for making high profit. In this regard, the dynamics and structure of foreign investments is an extremely important indicator of development of the country. Moreover, under the conditions of Georgia, when there are small amounts of domestic resources for development, budget resources are limited and savings of economic subjects are too small for investments. Inflow of foreign investments is not the only provision with financial resources; in the first place, this is an opportunity for sharing technological achievements, which is needed by the country. Besides this, direct investments have serious potential for employment. Subject to the long-term perspectives of development, in course forming an investment climate, the necessity of creating unified conditions of foreign and national investment activities shall be considered.

This is the axiom of economy, as investment activity and economic development of the country are in proportional relations. Therewith, there is a proportional relation between foreign direct investments and GDP growth.

After the crisis, attraction of foreign direct investments remains to be the main challenge of the Georgian Government. Reduction of direct foreign investments in many countries gave rise to serious macroeconomic problems. After the crisis, competition in attracting foreign direct investments became worse. While the country is unable to develop their own economy without assistance, foreign investments are of essential importance for economic growth of the country.

However paradoxical it may sound, the main problem of Georgia is the same as insufficient investments. Another and very important problem is high interest rates on loans. Few businesses can pay such high interest rates. These factors, of course, prevent development of the economy of the country and this is the main responsibility of the government and banking system together. The banks shall have healthy competition and they shall not agree "secretly" about high interest rates.

Table 4. GDP and Foreign Direct Investments

	2007	2008	2009	2010	2011	2012	2013	2014
GDP in current prices (million US Dollars)	10172	12801	10767	11663	14439	15830	16140	16529
Foreign Direct Investment (million US Dollars)	2015	1564	569	814	1117	912	942	1758
Share of Foreign Direct Investment in GDP (%)	20	12	6	7	8	6	6	11

Source: http://www.ndg.gov.ge/index.php?m=494.

Here the National Bank shall have its say. Under market conditions, the government shall create unified rules of game for every industrial subject. In relation with the banking sector, the Government is liable to have strict rules of regulation, which shall be processed, determined and monitored by banking supervision service. It shall also be noted that the main objective for management of commercial banks is making maximal profit and for this purpose, it may take on particular risks. Due to this, the government determines particular regulations to protect depositors, shareholders, investors, as well as economic stability and safety.

Another condition shall be emphasized as well – one of the most important problems of the Georgian economy and reforms is not only attraction of foreign investments, but also the direction of the mechanism of implementing investment strategy to the implementation of domestic investments of the country and new investment projects, as well as their practical use.

JSC State Investment Fund “Partnership Fund” established in 2011 plays a great role in implementation of large investments in Georgia today. It shall be noted that the Fund has been awarded rating BB- of international rating agency Fitch, which equals the credit rating of Georgia. Partnership Fund was created on the basis of consolidation of large governmental enterprises existing in the field of transport, energy and infrastructure. The main purpose of the Fund is promotion of investments in Georgia through participation at the initial stage of development of investment projects (co-investment in capital, subordinated loans, etc).

Activities of the Partnership Fund is implemented in two directions:

1. **Asset management** – total turnover of the assets existing in management of the fund in 2012 was more than 750 million US Dollars. Today, total volume of investment projects of the Fund is increased up to two thousand US Dollars. Portfolio of assets of the Fund includes the following components of strategic importance: Georgian Railway – 100% share; Georgian Oil and Gas Corporation – 100% share; Georgian State Electric System – 100% share; Commercial Operatory of Georgian State Electricity System – 100% share; JSC Telasi – 24.5% share. The Georgian Railway and Oil and Gas Corporation are the main source of funding of investment activities of the Partnership Fund.
2. **Investment activity** – today there are several projects in different sectors of economy in the portfolio of the Fund. The Fund is eligible to implement investments only in Georgia and its strategy is directed towards attraction and assistance of private investment.

It is important for the Fund to assist commercially profitable projects in sectors of Georgian economy, which are distinguished by great potential of development. This includes the following sectors: energy, agro-business, production, real estate and tourism, infrastructure and logistics. For funding, they consider only commercially purposeful projects, managed by experienced partners and employing specialized operators. The Fund renders financial partnership to private investors, expressed in average and long-term co-funding. It occupies the role of passive partner as in the projects of Greenfield (new business initiatives) and Brownfield (investment in existing business), with preliminarily determined exit strategies. Parallel to its participation in the Project, the Fund also assists in obtaining predominant funding for the project from commercial resources and international financial institutions. The funding is provided by the Fund by participating in the capital and in some cases, through subordinated loans (convertible and nonconvertible). Participation of the Fund in the projects shall not be more than 50% of the capital. Together with the funding, the Fund helps partner and manage the teams to achieve long-term sustainability [23].

The fund finances private investors by foreseeing the following conditions: the partnership fund may implement investments only in Georgia, in every sector except service field; the Fund implements investments only in commercially profitable projects; the Fund is eligible to participate in the capital and issue subordinated/predominant loans (both convertible and nonconvertible); the Fund's participation in the project, in the form of capital or loans, shall not be more than the share of private investors; the purpose of the Fund is participation in projects including the smallest co-shareholder, with middle or long-term perspective. When the project becomes sustainable, the Fund leaves the participation [24].

And generally, solving tasks of investment development of the country, for inflow of investments and partial stability of the exchange rate of Georgian Lari, is impossible on the basis of only such market, which is distinguished by low levels of formation in our economy. Strengthening the role of government, correction of economic policy, and seeking optimal conformity of market regulations is required. Therewith, borders and principles of state participation in the investment process shall be determined, taking into account specificity of economic development of Georgia, which characterizes the period of transfer to the market.

Monetary and Fiscal Policy Together Shall Serve Recovery of Georgian Lari

We shall leave the trend of mutual-blame established in Georgia:

> I have read somewhere; Georgian Lari is not a market product. It is the product of the central bank, consequently, it depends entirely upon the National Bank to stabilize or devalue it. Cases related with Georgian Lari have always involved political decisions. Moreover, in 2002, 2004 and 2007 every act related with Georgian Lari was always implemented in connection with political requirements.

I do not categorically agree with the said thesis.

In the first place, the problem of devaluation of national currency is a general problem, thus, everybody bears liability and is responsible for the faith of Georgian Lari and relatively, upon the faith of people and country. It is the duty of everybody including government, national bank, and legislative authorities to correctly plan structural and functional obligations; it is extremely important to monitor the entire banking system, National Bank, Supervisory Service ("deprived" or "seized"), even the parliament. The Parliament is the main conditioning body of financial-budgetary policy in the country and its obligation is to have particular supervision over these structures. The Parliament is responsible for the financial monitoring [27].

Another important thesis, or axiom, as I have already written about, is a very popular opinion in Georgia, regarding the fact that the Government shall not be involved in the activities of the industrial subject, though they often mix up intervention and prescribe necessary regulations. This opinion is shared by T. Basilia. He writes: “at the same time, under the conditions of market economy, the government shall create unified rules of game for every industrial subject, to protect competition, security and etc. In relation with the banking sector, the government is liable to have strict rules of regulation, processing, setting and monitoring the competence of banking supervision. Independence of the banking sector is not untouchable. Moreover, there is no untouchable sector in any democratic country – everybody is equal against the law. The government determined the rules of the game, which shall be protected by everybody, including the banking sector. For example, several months ago, the US Government brought charges to the management of five largest banks for criminal offense – Citigroup, JPMorgan Chase, Barclays and Royal Bank of Scotland and fined them 5.6 billion US Dollars for manipulating the exchange rate of currency. In Georgia, devaluation of Georgian Lari took place several months ago and nobody knows the real reason for that. I emphasize that the government shall not intervene with the activities of the banking sector. This is not the government’s business – the government shall look into the banking sector. These are different concepts.

The government shall use the banking supervision service in this process and make its work more beneficial. Actually there are problems in the banking sector of Georgia, and the Government is liable to learn this in a timely manner and take respective steps, in order to avoid serious cataclysms” [26].

It shall also be noted that we will not be able to use fiscal policy pursued by the government. I emphasize again that budgetary expenditures influenced greatly upon devaluation of Georgian Lari.

Amounts (mass) of Georgian Lari existed in the country significantly influenced upon the exchange rate of Georgian Lari, as the exchange rate is being formed with correlation of the masses of US Dollars and Georgian Laris. If the rate of growth of the mass of Georgian Lari is much more than the rate of growth of inflow of US Dollars, the exchange rate of Georgian Lari is devalued. One of the sources of increasing Lari is the deficit expense of sums from budget; i.e., when the government spends more funds, than it receives funds from the economy in the form of budgetary incomes in the same period.

In December of 2014, incomes of the state budget (including selling of non-financial assets) made 846 million Georgian Laris. This is the sum received by the government from the economy in December, as for the expenditures of state budget (including purchasing non-financial assets) made 1,110 million Georgian Laris. This is the volume of Lari "launched" by the Government into the economy in December.

As you can see, in December, 2014 there were more expenses in 264 (1 110-846) million Georgian Laris from the state budget, than incomes to the budget

In December, the National Bank increased refinancing loans by 200 million Georgian Laris. This is a one-week loan, which is given by the National Bank to the commercial banks for provision of short-term liquidity.

As we have mentioned above, strengthening the exchange rate of the national currency is supported with high rates of economic growth, as demand is being increased on the national currency. Herewith, it is important that economic growth shall be based on the growth of investments and not fiscal and monetary stimulation, such as deficit expenditures from the budget and increasing mass of Georgian Lari existed in circulation. The average rate of economic growth in Georgia in November-December of 2015 was 0.7%; and deficit spending of Lari from the budget and increasing loans of refinancing stimulated the economy.

Since January, 2015, existing factors of the devalued exchange rate of Georgian Lari (decreased flows of US Dollars, falling rate of economic growth, global appreciation of US Dollar) was added to the volume of increased Lari, created by deficit spending in the state budget. The Government didn't fulfill its condition announced in the statement by the President of the National Bank made in December 5, according to which, deficit spending of the budget would not be implemented. Consequently, the official rate of the Georgian Lari for January 28, 2015 was 2.06 against the US Dollar [28].

Today, we dream of this value: the exchange rate of Georgian Lari as of September, 2015 was 2.44. This is extremely hard for the Country.

Thus, incorrect planning of the budget, with its asymmetric and asynchronic nature on incomes and, especially, expenditures, gives rise to the periodic influx of mass cash into the economy, influencing inflation. The government faces political risks and challenges. The responsibility of the government is to manage industry, business and industrial environments.

Incorrect, irrational and extended bureaucratic expenditures, funding projects of doubtful public value, accessing regulation of business activities, nepotism – this is an incomplete list of the factors preventing business development, consequently, the growth of export potential and interest of foreign investors in the Georgian economy. All of these greatly damage the stability of the Georgian Lari, appreciating risk-factors decreasing its rate [29].

Neither the monetary fund, nor economic experts refute that the source of the problem related with Georgian Lari is conditioned basically with the external shock, although, another case is how effectively we use the existing instruments for the short-term and long-term periods inside the National Bank of the Country.

Short-term instruments are monetary instruments, owned by the National Bank and used less effectively. For example, according to the expert L. Kalandadze, there are particular currency shocks, localization and prevention of which may be provided with monetary instruments (they have the function of removing panic and shock effects) [27].

L. Qistauri too supports the regulation of the exchange rate of Georgian Lari with monetary instruments. He notes that the reason for the falling exchange rate is the absence of US Dollars in the market. Consequently, they increase US Dollars, or reduce Laris in circulation. There are no instruments for instant growth of Dollar mass. This is the problem of strategic work of the government. On the other hand, the National Bank uses promissory notes together with instruments for reducing the exchange rate of Lari named above (loans of refinancing, depository certificates, etc.) [25].

At the same time, we shall not diminish the role and "merit" of the National Bank in devaluation of Georgian Lari. Generally, the National Bank assumes direct institutional (and its management – personal) responsibility for inflation, and not the exchange rate of the Currency. At the same time, it is able not only to regulate the mass of money in circulation, but influence the price of credit resources, "implement" or strictly regulate opportunities of financial speculations, take measures in connection with formation of unhealthy resonance in the public, by launching/removing additional monetary reserves into/from circulation. Its acts may be justified only in context of providing a planned index of inflation – legislative casualties and the attempt of removing responsibility for monetary and financial stability faced by the countries for the National Bank. The National Bank is actually always facing a dilemma: to increase the monetary rate, reducing money mass in circulation several times, or to "care" for raising (about 20 percent) the extremely low level of monetizing Gross Domestic Product and for this purpose to issue additional money mass into the circulation. Though, reduction of money mass truly suppresses inflation, preventing its “imprudence,” it includes industrial danger, as well as that of business activity and rates of economic growth, money, expensing credit resources, and finally monetary anemia of the economy (money starvation). Due to this, if the policy of the National Bank directs sectorial interest only to one aspect of macroeconomic stability – low inflation (and not the strategy of economic growth – formally, this is the responsibility of the executive government...), we receive “tamed” inflation and low rates of economy [29].

It is extremely difficult to hear and accept the blame announced regarding the National Bank of Georgia, but I considered it necessary to recall certain arguments of blame, published by Georgian economists.

“Delays in national production, devaluation of incomes of producers and consumers, unbearable hardening of credit load, delays in economic growth, increasing deficits – this is an incomplete list of the outcomes, following non-consideration of the recommendation of the Monetary Fund and it will be followed in the future, if existing reality is not changed” [31].

According to the President of the Association of Young Financials and Businessmen, notwithstanding recommendations and demands of the Monetary Fund, the National Bank of Georgia did not form the mode of counter-cyclical capital buffers for the banking system. Besides this, it has not activated loan-to-value adequacy principle and payment-to income parity principle for the borrowers. Consequently, a difficult situation is created in the banking sector. Particularly, according to the requirements of National Bank of Georgia, commercial banks, being managed with the existed mechanism of calculating risks, cannot evaluate national production adequately.

Besides this, according to Mr. Chichinadze, subject to the regulations of the National Bank of Georgia and against requirements of the Monetary Funds, crediting uncovered requirements takes place, for example, issuing loans in US Dollar to the consumers, who have incomes in Georgian Lari. Transferring currency risks to the consumers is explained as follows.

This problem was clearly seen after currency fluctuations of the last period, when many citizens faced significantly increased loan obligations. This outcome was created by non-consideration of recommendations of the Monetary Fund by the National Bank.

“Instead of the fact that National Bank was limited in issuing uncovered loans, i.e., issuing loans in foreign currency to the persons, having income in Georgian Lari, its policy transferred currency risks entirely to the borrowers, who are not often aware in financial issues. National Bank in fact sacrificed such citizens and made them appear under hard currency risk, which was originated in November of last year and the citizens are paying loans becoming more expensive by 30-35%.

Though, according to the report of the Monetary Fund, the monetary policy of the national Bank is evaluated positively. Critics touch upon prudent management. Therewith, according to the Monetary Fund, the current adopted practice of monetary policy creates a positive outcome only under the conditions of a stable exchange rate, which doesn't touch upon today's state of the Georgian Lari. Consequently, the current policy of excess supply of Georgian Lari should be reviewed, as this makes the state of Lari more difficult," - writes Nodar Chichinadze [31].

Young financial managers consider that the National Bank of Georgia did not foresee other requirements of the Monetary Funds, particularly:

- Notwithstanding promise to the Monetary Fund, the National Bank of Georgia has not created a Board of Financial Stability, which shall form prudent regulation.
- Since 2012, the National Bank has not published reports of financial stability, which should be published on an annual basis according to the international standards as required by the Fund [31].

In conclusion, we shall note that the existing policy of the National Bank supports increasing consumer loans and, relatively, strengthening load of deficits, on the other side, the existing system of risk management prevents increasing activities in the industrial sector of banking institutions.

Inflation Expectations, Monetary Speculations and New Economic Dangers

Together with the objective reasons for dropping the exchange rate, I consider it necessary to emphasize one issue out of the objective reasons, and namely, incorrect evaluation made by some experts, accessing attention towards the media and often artificially aggravating the situation. Another reason for the drop in exchange rate is the panic, and overcoming this attitude, will assist stabilization of the exchange rate of Georgian Lari. Generally, immediate activities shall be undergone for termination of negative expectations for the business.

Blumberg's System is an absolutely closed system. I do not consider myself sufficient to criticize Blumberg's System, but I think I have the right to ask the question: what volumes are there in the transactions? What is demand-distribution of funds? Does this phenomenon give rise to the so-called inflation expectations? This latest may be worse than inflation itself. Inflation expectation is excess load and pressure on Georgian Lari. In such case, notwithstanding the fact that whether the bank customer needs currency or not, he/she keeps purchasing it anyway. This has quite negative outcomes.

I might overestimate my competence, but I consider it necessary to change the trade system and trade principles.

Any attempt of discrediting influences negatively upon it and outcome of such propaganda is always pitiful: nihilism is developed in population towards this currency and it is truly devalued. Thus, "prognosis" of devaluation of Georgian Lari may turn into reality, if Government is too late to take counter measures.

Professor Mikheil Tokmajisjvili shares the idea that it is dangerous to create expectations of currency devaluation: rate fluctuation is not in any country as deplorable as here in Georgia, where the economy is 'dedollarized'. If we assure the population that Lari will be truly devalued, the so-called crowd effect will be activated – when everybody tries to apply a currency exchange point and "save" his/her small savings or salary. For this reason, an excess amount of money is created at the market and the process is started, which is called "speculative effect" – the population massively purchases US Dollars and it drops the exchange rate of the national Currency. Due to this, the exchange rate of Georgian Lari shall become the subject of discussion of professionals and not politicians. When in summer opposition starts speaking about devaluing Georgian Lari in September, this is a huge mistake. If everybody who receives remuneration goes and purchases US Dollars, if hundreds and thousands of people behave so, can you imagine what may happen [21]?

Why is devaluation of Georgian Lari related with autumn? If we look through history, the most radical changes in exchange rates here happened in autumn: it happened in 1999, November 2008, and it happened last year. Economic activity is increased in autumn and demand on money is increased as well. Due to this, fluctuation of the exchange rate often happened in autumn. Though, we cannot blame any bank for devaluation of Georgian Lari. Though, in the case of uniting several banks, they will be able to influence the exchange rate, but this will be only one step having no long-term outcome. Due to this, I think that the bank cannot manage the exchange rate crisis, in course of discussing this problem, which shall be focused on the objective factors, such as: present state of economy, investments, export opportunities of the country, level of their utilization, etc.

As for the National Bank, it may freeze the exchange rate of Lari, but in such case, the economy stops entirely. Due to this, we shall select which is better: 1) to have Lari devalued smoothly and not in stages, and instead to stimulate development of the economy and 2) to stop the economy, and watch the Lari be stable and happy…

To my mind, Devaluation of Georgian Lari is not among the functions and interests of the National Bank: its main objective is to supply the economy with money and maintain a low index of inflation.

We live in the country of absurd: low rates of increasing real sector of economy, maximum dollarization of economy, sharp reduction trend of exports, turning into a country of imports, insufficient flows of investments, global financial crisis, appreciation of US Dollar worldwide, inflation expectations, significant reduction of cash transfers, foreign and domestic debts, unreasonable expenses of budget, foreign shocks independent from us, these were added with new arguments – excess debts of commercial banks…

Here is a long, but still incomplete list to be noted, analyzed, and foreseen for rescuing the Georgian monetary unit.

"In every normal country, the main "stadium" of forming exchange rate is the interbank market, as the banks are large sellers and purchasers of foreign currency. Consequently, the existing model for determining the exchange rate of Georgian Lari conforms to the international practice, though this doesn't exclude informal transactions between the largest players – the so-called market makers… As for small markets similar to the Georgian one, there are much more opportunities for informal transactions here, though it is in fact impossible to find actual data of their use" [32].

Banks determine the exchange rate of Georgian Lari with absolute secrecy at an interbank market in Georgia. The exchange rate of the National Bank shall be determined at an open and non-speculative market and the rate formed under such conditions shall be accepted by the Government and population to be objective datum.

It shall also be noted that in the developed countries (i.e., in Georgia as well), where there are weak economies, it is purposeful to use such exchange mechanisms, which will be transparent and formation of the exchange rate at the same time shall be subject to particular rules, which shall be known by everybody.

National Bank implements interventions as in Georgian Lari, so – US Dollars. Mainly, it shall feel the time and kind of funds needed. This is the issue of competence and professionalism. When fluctuation of the exchange rate is started, it is necessary to stop and decrease the exchange rate.

The National Bank holds the most effective mechanisms of regulation of the volume of currencies in the economy. One of them is the loan of refinancing issued by the National Bank to the commercial banks. The National Bank activated refinancing loans from September 2008 as the instrument of monetary policy. The purpose of similar loans is management of short-term interest rates at the interbank market. Except for short-term refinancing loans, the arsenal of the National Bank of Georgia includes standing refinancing loans. With help, commercial banks are able to raise guaranteed loans, without auction.

As you can see, refinancing loans are one of the real instruments owned by the National Bank of Georgia to increase or reduce (as needed) the volume of Georgian Lari in the economy. It is interesting that after changing governments in the Country, the volume of Georgian Lari in the economy is being sharply increased with the refinancing loans; if during the period of the National Movement the greatest volume of refinancing loan was 400 million US Dollars, in 2013-2014 such volume exceeds 500 million.

As I have already noted, regulation of devaluation of National Currency started in autumn 2014, and could be provided by reducing refinancing loans by the National Bank. It happened conversely, the volume of refinancing loans reached its historical maximum – 965 million Georgian Laris and it became the subject of hot discussions. The National Bank provides a collection of refinancing loans for guarantying the rate of monetary policy by using different instruments and in case of excess liquidity or/and it fills the deficit of liquidity with refinancing loans, i.e., it provides banks with resources.

Notwithstanding the fact that they are for one week, refinancing loans do not influence money mass, as they are reissued on weekly basis, and the main thing is that the volume of refinancing loans is being permanently increased during the last period. I.e., if National Bank issues to the commercial banks, for example, 100 million Georgian Laris, it increases the money mass a single time. If increasing the volume of a loan doesn't take place, every following return will not influence money mass within 100 million. Though, when increasing the balance of refinancing loans, this also influences money mass. This is exactly what happens today during the last period. For example, in 2013, the balance of refinancing loans was increased 36 million Georgian Laris and by the end of the year it made 400 million Georgian Laris (during the year it was below 1 million Georgian Lari), in 2014, the balance was increased from 400 to 712 million Georgian Lari, and during the current year it has increased up to 965 million. I.e., during the last year, volume of refinancing loans has been increased almost half a billion Georgian Lari. Thus, the argument of "one-week" of refinancing loans is less reasonable.

By means of analyzing facts, we accepted the following image: banks receive governmental securities (request of bans is more than delivery of securities in 2-3 times), i.e., they borrow money to government and then for filling liquidity they appeal to the National Bank, i.e., borrow from the National Bank. More briefly, commercial Banks borrow from the National bank and lend to the Government.

The financial side of this scheme is important as well – commercial banks receive loans from the National Bank of Georgia at an average of 4.5%, and lend it to the government for 6%, 7%, 10% and 11% according to the maturity, i.e., they find quite solid, tens of millions of interest income in Georgian Lari [34].

Under the conditions of problems with Georgian Lari, permanent growth of refinancing loans plays a negative role; when the National Bank announced their intent to strengthen the monetary policy. Though, this decision has been expressed in only 50 basis points of the rate of monetary policy, which doesn't change reality.

The banking sector, being accustomed to the "generosity" of the National Bank, invests excess liquidity into the securities of the government and makes a profit, and the National Bank fills the deficit, which pressures Georgian Lari. National Bank of Georgia seems not to strengthen monetary policy. Though, it shall be noted that issuance of standing refinancing loans, fixed twice in current year, may be considered from the side of the National Bank of Georgia to be strengthening the monetary policy (as National Bank didn't provide banks the liquidity requested by them in full extent with the rate of monetary policy, and the banks paid over 1% for borrowing additional resources – i.e., they borrowed it at higher cost).

There is the situation that maintenance of the exchange rate of existing refinancing, for which the National Bank is careless about refinancing resources, is in its best interests, which means reaching the index of 5% purposeful inflation. Thus, the National Bank does not strengthen monetary policy, but it pursues minimum maintenance of soft monetary policy; National Bank of Georgia increases delivery of Lari by redemption of depository certificates and delivery of refinancing loans, with which it reaches a purposeful level; as for the Lari, it keeps dropping.

We consider it necessary to direct refinancing loans, as additional credit mass existed in the economy, not to be directed towards the monetary or consumer crediting market, but business funding.

This touches upon the situation; when the National Bank issues treasury liabilities and makes excess cash from the economy. I think you will agree that this is not a popular method. The main thing is, where the funds attracted with treasury liabilities will be directed. If they are directed towards state expenditures, this will have a negative effect, but if this is directed towards important profitable products, this, of course, will give impulse to the economy.

According to the data of the National Bank, as of March 31, 2015, Georgian Banks had immediate payment of 835 million US Dollars for its foreign creditors. Immediate payables include overdue debts and depository liabilities of every type to non-residents, notwithstanding maturity of deposits. I don't think anybody needs an explanation of what overdue debt means. Only this fact is enough for the Government to be interested in what happens in the Georgian banking sector; why Georgian banks have overdue debt owed to their foreign creditors and if the stability of banking system is in danger.

Generally, during the year 2015, Georgian banks shall pay their foreign creditors about 1.4 billion US Dollars. During following year 2016 – 506.7 million, and in 2017 the sum to be paid is increased by four and reaches 2 billion US Dollars.

Of course, interbank credits, opening credit lines by the international organizations and foreign banks are ordinary bank operations, but after introducing the data of the national bank there are questions about the Georgian banking system. Particularly, what is the debt of the banking sector to the foreign creditors? – 27 billion US Dollars. I.e., the Georgian banking sector attracted 2.7 billion US Dollars from abroad and shall return 4.4 billion, which is 1.4 billion US Dollars more than the principle sum. As we can see, this debt is 50% more than the service cost of the debt. Naturally, this gives rise to the question – what was the interest rate of the funds "borrowed" by the Georgian banking sector from foreign creditors? We know well that neither foreign banks, and moreover, nor – international organizations – have such "interest rates." Where has such catastrophic distinction originated?

According to one of the versions, the reason may be that the Georgian banking sector is unable to serve these debts with the agreed schedule, it cannot pay the sum to be paid in a timely manner, and due to this they have accumulated overdue liabilities, giving sharp rise to the interest rate and, relatively, expenses of the debt service. If this is the real reason, there is the question – why is the Georgian banking sector unable to pay debts without delays? What are the problems faced by them?

Particularly, if in July 2012 this debt was 2 billion US Dollars, as I have already said above, it makes 2.7 billion, i.e., it has increased 700 million US Dollars.

This phenomenon also may endanger macroeconomic stability of the country. Subject to the data of the national Bank, during the current year the country shall pay 3.8 billion US Dollars in the form of service of foreign debt (principle sum and accrued interest); including 221 million to be paid by the governmental sector, and the National Bank – 14.2 and banking sector – 1.4 billion US Dollars. And this happens when reserves of the National Bank is 2.5 billion US Dollars. I.e., the country shall pay 3.8 billion US Dollars, when reserves of the National Bank make only 2.5 billion (i.e., less than 1.3 billion US Dollars).

Is this dangerous for macroeconomic stability? Of course, it is. How is the National Bank going to cover this distinction and at the expense of what? Where does it plan to increase foreign currency into the country, to make it possible to take foreign obligations, in a way not endangering macroeconomic stability? These are the questions, which should be asked at the Parliament of Georgia, when they considered the principle direction of monetary-credit policy submitted by the National Bank, and management of the National Bank shall give public answers on these questions.

The Georgian banking system has already overcome a hard period, when after the war of Russia-Georgia of 2008 and due to the global financial crisis, Georgian banks had accumulated important foreign financial liabilities, it is noteworthy that during this period the entire Georgian banking system received assistance of 1.105 billion US Dollars from international financial organizations. Is there a possibility to repeat the same scenario in the future and why did the banking system repeat or not repeat mistakes?

In the first place, I do not want the same scenario to be repeated, as Georgia received this assistance for alleviation of the outcomes of war after 2008. Actually, the opportunity for repeatedly receiving such huge assistance from the international commonwealth is less possible. As for the assistance to the banking sector, this was the decision of the government of Georgia in those times, in order to avoid collapse of the banking system, approved by the international commonwealth. It is noteworthy that assistance to the banking sector was not a gift, grant – this was the loan issued for preferential conditions.

Chapter 7

Brief History of Origination of Georgian Money

Origination of Money

Money has a long history just like civilization of humanity. Monetary units changed with the centuries. Money has own history in separate countries and each of them is unique.

Initially, this was simple exchange in kind. Replacement of primitive activities of a human – hunting and foraging with more effective activity gave rise to the need of exchange of commodities, having the name of "barter."

Growth of the kinds of exchanging products, their perishability and provisional losses conditioned complication of operation of exchange in kind. Finding a companion, who would benefit from exchanging the offered goods with ones own, took much time. This was the reason humans were unsatisfied with exchange in kind, i.e., barters, and they decided to invert such universal means of payment, in exchange of which it would be possible to get goods and service of any kind.

They inverted and implemented. It was money (it comes from Latin Follis – a small bag, sack to keep 40 Numis – copper coins).

Commodity Money

The Latin name of money, Pecunia, comes from the word Pecun, which means 'herd.' While at the territory of modern Germany there was a monetary unit, herd (cow), to the northern people thc deer performed this function. Different nations in different eras recognized different units for money, such as: elephant Shuang, gem, animal fur, opium, cocoa, pearls, etc. Shells are best known, though many people considered slaves to be the measurement for price and payments. Though, such monetary units had multiple negatives. It was impossible to separate them (for example, cows) and transformation (for example, stones). Due to their heaviness and perishability, they could not be used several times. Therewith, the most important problem remained to obtain and store such money for long periods of time and without physical expenditures. Due to this, man used clear thinking and invented units much easier to transfer, more convertible, exchangeable, and usable for long periods of time than natural money – it was coins.

The Most Ancient Coins

The very first coins are thought to have appeared in China and Old Lydia Kingdom in the 7th century BC. In about 500 BC, Persian King Darius made an "Economic Revolution" in his Kingdom, involving coins as the official exchange unit and replaced barter with it. The coins were rapidly distributed in neighboring, barbarian tribes, and later farther and farther. In those times, only rich landowners and monasteries had sources and opportunities for minting coins. From the beginning, the coins were only of gold, silver or their alloys.

Though, soon, lack of precious metals conditioned minting coins from copper and bronze. They had no "internal" value, different from the precious metals, but they had respective signs reflecting values.

Modern Coins

You can distinguish the front side – obverse and back side – reverse at almost every coin. Each era used to leave particular traces on the types on the coin. On the ancient coins, you will notice only simple grooving. From the 5th century BC, digits and letters denoting denominations appeared (they expressed initials of cities with letters, where they were mint). And Darius was the first to forge his face on the coins. After this, they imaged on the coins nobles, heroes, historic events and lots of interesting facts.

Coins are actively used today in the commercial-financial system.

Banknotes

Prototype of the first paper money was created in China in the beginning of the 9th century. Large and important transactions required large sums of money, and for this the Empire printed paper of high quality, with signs on them. Paper was used instead of 10,000 copper coins. Massive printing of banknotes started in 1024, because financing war required large funds. This could not be provided with coins, due to their limited number and difficulty of transportation. Marco Polo wrote that issuance of banknotes was a new opportunity for achievement of the goal aspired by the alchemists. These opinions were provoked by imperial banknotes met by him during his travel to China in 1276. Chingis Khan's government freely exchanged these banknotes on gold.

Banknotes appeared in Europe relatively later. In 1661, Stockholm’s private emission bank printed the first official banknotes in Europe. Before that, Europeans had used promissory notes. This was a short- or long-term agreement between two parties obliging its (promissory note) issuer to pay the preliminarily agreed sum at the agreed time.

It is also noteworthy that in some countries they issued banknotes periodically and then removed them from the currency system. The reason for this was that when the government needed money, it was printing securities in large amounts, which were soon used to give rise to hyperinflation and they returned to metal again.

In 1945, to leave the crisis provoked by the Second World War and stimulation of international economic system, the so-called Bretton-Woods System was created in Bretton Woods. It gave rise to the “predominance” of the US Dollar in the international commercial and tax system, where the British Pound had occupied the leader’s position till 1914.

Before 1971, holders of banknotes were eligible to exchange paper money any time for gold in the bank according to the market price (gold standard). This meant that in the repository of the bank there should be gold of the amount conforming to the price of the emitted banknotes. In 1971, on the basis of international agreement, the banknotes lost the right; though some countries implemented this process after the First World War. Since then, paper money is not bound to any metal and it is freely used in the monetary system of the world [36].

At the Beginning of Turnover of the First Georgian Money

Here scientifically certified opinions about origination of Georgian money of V. Chantladze is of great interest here. They called money “Safase” (for price) earlier. According to the studies of the Academician Iv. Javakhishvili, the Georgian term Fuli (money) comes from Parisian word, which, in its turn comes from Greek.

Before the Hellenistic Era in the 6-4th centuries BC in Iberia, there were coins, though they were not circulated. There is the opinion that the principle equivalent those times was the seal. Even the people from Middle East, who were involved in the statehood and commercial activities, did not have coin systems in those times.

They used the term “Falling dram” for the term denoting minting money. “We “fell down” the dram with the image of the King Artashan in the city here” [37].

Turnover of Georgian coins of this period may be divided into two periods: the first – turnover of Colchis Tetri (VII-II centuries BC) and the turnover of other coins (III century BC and III century AD).

The coins – so-called Colchis Tetri – were circulated in Colchis in the beginning. The Coins were mint from silver by the Colchis King Aristarchus. He lived in the 1st century BC. The coins were mint in large and small numbers. Great amounts of such coins were found at the territory of ancient Colchis. Colchis Tetri was distributed in west Georgia. Colchis Tetri was not circulated in west Georgia from the 3rd century BC. From this period, the money of Persian Arshakunians (money of Archak IV Mithridates and his heirs) were circulated.

After the Romans entered, Denarius was distributed in Georgia. Later, Georgians started minting money similar to the Romans. In the 3rd century, Persians (Sasanians) mint Drachm from pure silver, which was widely distributed in Georgia. Roman Denarius Parthian Drachm was also circulated, most of which were found in east Georgia, and not in the west. Each Parthian coin had Greek legends. In VI-IV centuries BC, gold, silver and copper coins of Achaemenid dynasty were circulating in Iberia. At the territory of the Kingdom of Kartli, the round coin of Hellenistic Era was found. Imitation of Alexander the Macedonian’s gold coin was also minted here. Imitations of Macedonian Staters ware also found. They are basically found in total parts bordering Iberia. Gold Stater of Alexander the Great, Drachm, copper coin of the Government of Hellenistic Egypt Ptolemy VI Philometor, copper coins of Seleucids, Syrian kings, and coins of Mithridates VI of Pontus and others were also found here [38].

On the coastline of west Georgia imitations of Lysimachus' Staters were found. They belong to the 3rd century BC. Silver coins looking similar to Colchis Tetri were also found, which were minted in the 2nd part of the II century BC. According to D. Kapanadze and K. Golengo, these coins are related with the images of the coins of King Aristarchus.

PURCHASING CAPACITY OF THE FIRST GEORGIAN MONEY

We know only the prices of the antique market, according to which the most expensive slave cost and their prices started from 50-60 Drachms. Ox cost 10 Drachms, amphora of wine – 10-12 Drachms, shoes – 8 Drachms, daily remuneration of laborer – 1 Drachm. Economic relations were quite intensively developed in the Greek world through the Black Sea. This was expressed in the fact that the Georgian city Dioscurias issued their own money in the 1st century BC. These were city coins of Dioscurias – ancient Sokhumi. Notwithstanding their issuing in small numbers, i.e., equivalent of coins, the existence of city coins spoke of high economic development of Dioscurias. Besides this, golden coins of Alexander the Great, Roman Dinars and Parthian silver Drachms were also circulated here.

Coins of Davit the Builder and King Tamar's reign are also noteworthy. One important phenomenon was identified in this period, which was called the Silver Crisis. The states neighboring Georgia, Asia Minor and the Byzantine Empire were involved in the Silver Crisis. We were part of this world and notwithstanding the Golden Age, no silver coin was minted from David till Rusudan. From the history of the united Georgian Kingdom of the 10th century, the coin of David IV the Builder is the most impressive, the original of which is preserved in the London Museum. David with his entire royal glory is imaged on the Coin, and on the reverse side, there is the legend: "King of Kings of the Abkhazians, Kartvelians, Ranians, Kakhetians and the Armenians." The Silver crisis and long-term circulation of copper coins gave rise to irregular mintage of coins.

Mintage of coins from copper is much more difficult technologically, than minting silver. The strengthening economy and development of trading formed the need for mintage of larger amounts of money. This lost form of money, though, in those times, they struck copper coins of proper strike. The coins of irregular strike often lacked denoting of numbers, though it was in the cost of the silver money – Dirham. For example, on the coin of irregular strike issued in the reign of the King Tamara there is the legend: "Present Dirham was struck."

It was engraved on the head side of the silver coin struck during the reign of David III Kuropalate: "Jesus, Save David," and on the reverse there is the cross and Georgian legend: "Kurapalate." This is one of the rarest Georgian coins, included into international circulation. There are only four coins discovered and all four were found abroad. One of them was found in Germany at the city of Schwann, another in 1878 in Saint-Petersburg, the third one – in the 1900s in Estonian city Vila, and the fourth in Sweden. This coin confirms commercial-economic relations of Georgia with European countries in X-XI centuries.

During the reign of Heraclius II of Georgia, the coin business was at its highest level. The King activated own ores, where he settled Pontus Greeks and started mining Georgian metal. Every coin of silver or copper struck during his reign was made in the metal extracted in the south of Georgia, in the area of Borchalo. On the coins of Heraclius II a fish was engraved, which was the most ancient Christian symbol, also the state emblem of Bagrationi in those times. During the reign of Heraclius II of Georgia, they struck Sirma Abazi in Georgia. Except Georgia, these coins were circulated in Azerbaijan, Armenia and Dagestan. Notwithstanding the fact that since 1801 authority of Russian Empire was set up in Georgia, the coins struck during the reign of Heraclius II remained in circulation until 30s of the 19th century, provoked with his reliability. Besides this, the metal that the coins were made of was different in 98% clearness, being a firm money unit itself. During the reign of Heraclius II of Georgia, "Erekle's Chervonets" were also struck. In scientific literature, this coin is described as the coin of light discrepancy, because the date on the head side doesn't coincide with the reverse. It was not in wide circulation and only ten originals are reposted in the Georgian National Museum.

On the head side of the copper coin of Prince David of Georgia, there is peacock imaged and the date of Islamic calendar: 1215. On the reverse of the coin, there is the legend: "Tiflis." In 1801, after the death of the King of Kartli and Kakheti George XII of Georgia, Russia violated the Tractate of 1783 and annihilated Kartli-Kakhetian Kingdom. According to the prescribed rules, the son of King George should be ascended to the throne, but the Russians prevented this. Notwithstanding the fact that Prince David of Georgia was not the king, he struck the coin recognized to be the rarest Georgian coin. Its only example is known. It is reposted in the Berlin Museum.

TIME AND PLACE OF ORIGINATION OF THE FIRST COINS

Creation of coins is the revolution in the issue of economic development. Before creation of the money, various goods played the function of money, which were called ‘Saqonelfuli’ (commodity-money). This could be livestock, precious metal bar, copper bracelets, tools, etc.; though creation of struck money was related with the necessity of elimination of defects of ‘Saqonelfuli.’ Their storage and transportation were related with particular difficulties.

The merchant should have in his pocket or on the carriage new value for purchasing much. The bars could not play such function, moreover – the livestock. There appeared the necessity of having a more compact means of payment, of small size, small weight and very precious. Due to this, they focused on the precious metals, as they were obtained in small amounts in nature. Their non-deteriorating features may be named as the second reason for selection of the precious metal for money.

Thus, it was decided to select rare metals with high consumption price, i.e., purchasing capacities, for means of payment. Coins appeared in the seventh-sixth centuries BC. Creation of money is assigned to two locations: one of them is Aegina Island in the Aegean Sea and another, the Asianic state Lydia, situated, roughly saying, to the west of modern Ankara.

Let us return to Georgia. As we have said above, we may include Colchis into the list of the Pioneers creating the coin. In the sixth century BC, the colonists from the town Miletus, situated on the east coast of Aegean Sea, were settled here. They established Greek Town Phasis – modern Poti, Dioscurias – modern Sokhumi, Gyenos – modern Ochamchire, Pitiunt – modern Pitsunda. Phasis Greeks started mintage of coins in our territory.

This money was generally called Colchis Tetri and it was struck in the 1st-3rd centuries BC. This money was being circulated here and it is an affiliation of our culture as settled Greeks were gradually assimilated here. They became bilingual and speak earlier forms of Mengrelian together with the Greek language.

On the first coins, there were images only on one side. The coin has two sides – obverse and reverse. On the obverse side, they had images and on the other side, there was a sealed square shape. This was a characteristic feature of ancient coins.

Modern coins have two seals. They place metal on one seal and then press it with another. There was no second seal in those times. To put metal into the first seal, they took a special copper stick and wattle and pressed it against the seal. The square shape of the top wattle was engraved in the metal. Due to this, one side of the coins used to be more loaded with images than the reverse side. Later they guessed that they needed seals on the other side as well. There were lions and bulls imaged on Lydian coins. Aeginian coins had turtles on then, as Aegina meant 'turtle.'

As for the Colchis Tetri, there are eight types of them that reached us. They have a roaring lion, as well as a lying hermaphrodite lion. On the reverse side in the engraved square, a kneeling goddess with a bull head is imaged. On the Colchis Tetri they also imaged three human heads – on the obverse side there was one head and on the reverse – two heads facing each other in the engraved square shape. This is the moon goddess and three phases of the moon. Image of the human head is Greek-archaistic style. On one coin, there was the image of a crane.

The most popular type of Colchis Tetri is the coin with types of human and bull heads. These coins were the most distributed and the amount of them found in the west Georgia allowed their use as gunpowder in hunting in the second part of the nineteenth century.

As for the symbolism of the types, the bull was related with the worship of moon, and the lion – worship of the sun.

APPEARANCE OF GEORGIAN SYMBOLS ON THE MONEY STRUCK IN GEORGIA

First, the cross appears on the coin at the end of the sixth century, on the numismatic monuments of the presiding Prince Stephen I of Iberia. This was the noble, who built Jvari Monastery and obtained independence from Persians. His predecessor princes had struck coins similar to Sasanian versions, with the types of the Shah on the obverse side and the fire lit on the altar and two guardians on the reverse side. This is the pure Sasanian numismatic monument.

Princes of Kartli first imaged ancient Georgian alphabetical (Asomtavruli) signs ahead of the Shah's head. For example 'გ' (G) and 'ნ' (N) ('გურგენი',

Gurgen), or 'ჯ' J and 'რ' R ('ჯუანშერი', Juansher). Later Stephen I of Iberia removed fire from the reverse of the coin and imaged a cross instead of it and placed the full name 'სტეფანოზ' (Stephan) with Asomtavruli script.

Later David the Kouropalates imaged his numismatic monument with allusion: "God Save David the Kouropalates" and the cross on the coin. This is the Georgian symbol.

The coins were often engraved with the titles of kings. For example, King Giorgi was the King of Abkhazians and Kartvelians, and Nobilissimus, and Sebastos and Caesar, and in this regard, the union of Georgia was symbolically imaged on the numismatic monument of David the Builder's reign.

Bagrationi's emblem, developed by Heraclius II of Georgia, appears on his numismatic monument, where there are one- and two-headed eagles.

Imaging Common Eras on the Coins

Dates on the Georgian coins are counted differently. Some of them are counted according to the reigns; on some of them there are Muslim eras, as during particular periods, Arabs were on mintage coins in Kartli. It is the Hijri Calendar, which started from the day when Islamic prophet Muhammad and his followers escaped from Mecca to Medina. If our year follows the son, the Arab year follows the moon.

First Georgian chronology Choronikon was fixed on the numismatic monument of the George III of Georgia. His coin is also interesting as the first appearance of Mkhedruli script on it.

Reflecting the Presence of Invaders on Numismatic Monuments in Georgia

In this regard, the heaviest period was from the thirteenth through eighteenth centuries. Occupation coins were being struck during that period. Due to this, Tbilisi mint had a double load – in one and the same mint Mongols were minted coins together with Demetrius on behalf of Ilkhan seating in Iran. Abas struck in Isfahan were at the same time minted at the territory of Tbilisi.

STABILITY OF WORK OF GEORGIAN MINT

In the sixth-third centuries BC, Colchis Tetri was minted at the territory of Colchis in west Georgia. From the third century BC, new coins were struck instead of Colchis Tetri. As for the period of dominical year, no coins were being struck in west Georgia from the first till the tenth century. I.e., till the period when the Center moved to the east and not only to western Georgia, but to the entire territory of Georgia.

Such fall may be explained with the following phenomenon: a great amount of Byzantine money entered West Georgia and local money was not being struck. In west and east Georgia it became a common economic and political domain, Bagrat the 4th strike coins.

Colchis started minting money well, though later it had a huge fall from the first till the tenth century of the new era. As for east Georgia, it happened the other way. Coins seemed not to be minted in Iberia. It was started relatively late, in the third century BC, though it continued more steadily.

The first real coins were struck in the third century, BC by Bagrat the son of Biurat. This was the prince of Klarjeti, the first Bagrationi. Coins struck after this were minted by false moneyers. They imitated the imitations entered from Colchis. In the fourth-fifth centuries, no coins were struck in Iberia. In the sixth century they were struck by the princes of Kartli. In the seventh century, they didn't mint money, and in the eighth century, coins of Muslim type were struck by Arabs.

Tbilisi Mint works intensively in the eighth, ninth, and tenth centuries. This is where mintage of coins is stopped and west Georgia is activated in this regard. Coins of Bagrat the IV, Giorgi the II and David the Builder were minted in Kutaisi. Demetrius the first, Giorgi the second and Tamar minted millions of coins in Tbilisi, after this minting money was not in fact stopped at the territory of east Georgia, though the coins could be national and occupational series – of Mongols, Iranians, and later from 1804 – of Russians.

As for west Georgia, coins were struck periodically here in the Middle Ages; for example, David Ulu escaped to Davit Narin in Kutaisi. They struck coins. Rusudan escaped to Tskhumi and they struck coins there, etc. In the XVII-XVIII centuries, no coins were minted in west Georgia. Large silver European coins and very small Ottoman Akçes in purses were entering.

Georgian numismatic stopped in 1832-33, when the Russian Mint was closed in Tbilisi. Russians struck coins, circulated here. Then problems occurred and minting money was completely stopped.

APPEARANCE OF PAPER MONEY IN GEORGIA

During Russian rule, paper money enters Georgia. It is already bonistics. Paper money considered 0.8 g of was gold stored at the National Reserve Bank. Georgians understood this less and could not understand the sense of paper money in the nineteenth century.

Russian money entered in two categories; one was allowances without support of gold. Later banknotes supported with gold [39].

GEORGIAN MONEY TODAY

The First Georgian Paper Banknotes to Georgia

In 1918, after gaining independence by our country, the Georgian Republic started thinking about creation of its own currency. This is a very difficult and extended process and in 1919 temporary means for payment – Georgian Boni was issued. The right of emission of Georgian currency was the prerogative of the Ministry of Finance in those times. Due to this, there are the facsimiles of the Minister of Finance of Georgia Konstatine Kandelaki and Chairman of the Government Noe Zhordania applied to the banknotes. The Georgian state emblem was printed on Georgian Bonis, as the symbol of the Republic of Georgia. On December 31, 1919, the State Central Bank of Georgia, the legal assign of the National Bank was established, first chairman of which was the financier and lawyer Jason Lortkipanidze, brother of famous writer Niko Lortkipanidze.

The Georgian government was working on creation of National Currency as well. They had a name as well. It should be named Marchili. Famous artist Evgeni Lansere was painting a sample of one of the coins, which is reposted at the National Museum, though due to the famous events, they had no time for emission of Marchili.

Importance of Involving Coupons in Georgia

We shall refer to Sh. Qistauri's words: "National currency, national monetary unit will be involved and enhanced in turnover only in case of respective preconditions. There are three main conditions determining them:

political, economic and social. In its turn, all three conditions, each separately include quite a large complex of activities, which are necessary to be pursued in life not for putting money into circulation, but also for its establishment and further strengthening, and effective functioning of monetary system."

Out of political conditions, the existence of a strong government built on independent and democratic origins is the most important (legislative, executive, judiciary), as well as authority of the government in public and calmness in the country.

Out of economic conditions, inviolability and safety of private property (private, state, collective or personal) are the most important, as well as growth of production and reasonable and moderate state management of respective financial-credit, tax, customs, tariff and other polices."

Creation and strengthening of a firm own currency, moreover, its formation and establishment as a system (monctary-currency system), except political and economic provisions, requires respective social provision, existence of such layers of people, which will be in close relation with monetary-commodity relations, functionality of the economy with its interests and activities [42].

Involving own money in Georgia when the country was involved in the civil war and the economy was absolutely paralyzed, even in case of existence of the Three Conditions, was related with great problems. In this regard, the main and the most acute issue is provision of newly issued money with commodity funds. Moreover, if mass of respective commodities were not provided, newly issued Georgian money would be devalued again, similar to the soviet money. What was the situation in this regard in our republic? Too hard. Due to the fact that economy of the Republic did not actually work (only in 1992, compared to previous years, productiveness of industry and agriculture was reduced 45-55%), provision of monetary units with its own forces with commodity funds was absolutely impossible. Histories of inflation liquidation and involvement of own currency does not know of any case of having the economy paralyzed, inflation reaching astronomic figures where a particular country could implement involvement of a new currency and its implementation. As a rule, this took place with foreign credits, assistance, subsidies and creation of respective economic funds and nature with the newly issued currencies. This is what the Federal Republic of Germany did in 1948, when it involved its own banknotes; England – in 1949 in course of implementing devaluation of pound sterling, France – when involving "heavy franc" in 1958, etc. Each of them took billions of credits from the USA, International Monetary Fund, international banks, various countries... West

Germany of those times, by implementing money reform, did not only make a foundation toward its state independence, but also separated its economy from the degraded structures of the eastern block (revived its economy, of course, by activation of internal levers). For this, West Germany received from the USA credit more than 17 billion US Dollars, 3.7 billion US Dollars from England, 600 billion US Dollars – from France. If West Germany, which had much more favorable conditions than we had (in many aspects, it was under conditions similar to ours), needed investment of tens of billions of US Dollars for involvement of its currency and revival of the country, we will definitely need this source of funding. Japan, South Korea, Israel and other countries, used the same methods and means for issuing and improving their currencies and economic development after World War Two.

We had not declared independence yet, when there were wide discussions in media and various verbal publications about issuance of the Georgian national currency and its possible names. The first article was published in the June 24, 1990 issue of the Newspaper Republic. The author of the article, together with justification of political, economic and social conditions offered naming of Georgian currency national name (opinions of the same author, about necessary issuance of Georgian money and its name, published in wider form in the June issue of the same year of the magazine, the Economist). Later, multiple articles and letters of various authors were published in various magazines, newspapers, collections, booklets and books about issuance of Georgian money, its economic and political provision, conversion, name, etc.; it was broadcasted on Radio and TV shows; said at various scientific and economic meetings.

Abundance of letters, opinions and applications touched upon the name for Georgian money. This was understandable, “national currency, national banknote were similarly necessary and essential attributes for the people standing on the road of complete independence, as national anthem, flag and emblem” and, respectfully, it should be national in form and name. The authors offered various names, which should be given to the future Georgian money. There were academicians and professors, docents and scientific workers, post-graduate students, students, ordinary citizens and many others among authors. One part of them thought Georgian Lari should be named Marchili, others – Tetri; one part of them thought not to change anything and live the name Ruble, and its hundredth part – Kopek. There were suggestions to give national currency the name Kolkha, Iberi, Lari.

Since the first days of gaining independence Georgia, and its National Forces, tried not to take Georgia out of the imperial domain, but also to take it from commanding-administrative system to the democratic system of management, market system, to create and develop a national economy, strengthen the political state of the country inside and outside Georgia, to improve social life and many other issues, though they could not make actual results. It was understandable: by that time, Georgia had no strong lever of economic, political and social construction, such as a national banknote, or national currency. Instead of it, Rubles of the Metropolis (Russian Federation) were being circulated in Georgia, which had left the Empire and declared independence.

In the 90s, deficits of banknotes were formed in Georgia and the population could not receive salaries, pensions, assistances, or various payments for months and years. All these gave rise to discontent of wide masses of population, destruction of institutional power, non-fulfillment of business obligations by the employees and many others. In January-February of 1993 the Metropolis, in fact, stopped distribution of the Ruble to Georgia. Notwithstanding multiple telephone and written requests and appeals from the side of the Georgian government, the Russian Federation did not issue banknotes. When the situation became catastrophic, in 1993, the Head of the Government of those times, Eduard Shevardnadze, appealed to President of Russia Boris Yeltsin in an open letter (published in media), where it was emphasized that, according to the agreement, Russia should provide Georgia with the banknotes (Rubles), which should make a colossal value – 60 billion Rubbles by March 1, 1993, due to which population failed to receive salaries, pensions, assistances and other payments for months and years; this gave rise to discontent of people, anti-governmental protests, demonstrations, meetings and etc. By publishing this letter to Yeltsin, the Georgian government seems to try to influence the President of Russia, but it could not do anything… No Rubles were delivered to Georgia.

Under such conditions, the Government, which had had quite sensible relations with the International Monetary Fund, World Bank, US Administration and Western countries and structures, made the decision (there was no way out), to issue its own banknotes immediately, and on April 5, 1993 it issued its own taxation and settlement means – Coupon.

From April 5, 1993 the Coupon was issued in 5, 10, 50, 100, 500, 1000, 5000, 10000. It shall be noted that at the beginning, the Russian and USSR Ruble was left in the circulation, making serious problems to establishment of coupons and affected the maintenance of the exchange rate of the Coupon. Though, in July 1993, Russia excluded from circulation the banknotes issued before 1993, but this did not influence termination of devaluation of the coupon; on the contrary, necessity of their exchanges for coupons gave serious stress.

The coupon exchange rate against the Ruble was one to one (USD-GEL: 1-1000 Coupons) at issuance, began devaluation soon. This was understandable, due to the paralyzing economy, catastrophic growth of budget deficit (in 1992, 1993, 1994 deficits of republic and local budgets made 80-95%), unprecedented price explosion and many other factors, newly issued national banknotes – the Coupon was left without any economic and political provision. Consequently, every attempt of the National Bank to stop devaluing the coupon, failed. The situation was complicated by the fact that civil war and later ethnic conflicts, war in Abkhazia and Samachablo, gave rapid rise to the military and other expenses of the government, the only source of repayment of which was increasing the issuance of money. Archive materials of the National Bank show increasing rates of Coupon circulation. In the 2nd quarter of 1993, 96.7 billion Coupons were issued into circulation; in the 3rd quarter of 1993 – 192.7 billion Coupons; in the 1st quarter of 1994 – 767 billion Coupons; in the 2nd quarter of 1994 there was application for 1.7 trillion coupons, though, due to the fact that the National Bank actually had no coupons of sufficient amount (coupons issued into circulation were not returned to the banks due to the paralyzing economy), besides only 948.0 billion coupons were issued; in the 3rd quarter of 1994 they foresaw issuance of 2.5 trillion coupons into circulation.

Subject to the issuance of increasing amounts of coupons into circulation, the exchange rate against the US Dollar was increasingly falling. If on April 5, 1993, 1 US Dollar cost 1,000 coupons; on July 1 – it was 4,800 coupons; on October 5 – 12, 624 coupons; on January 1, 1994 – 102,900 Coupons and on September 1 – 5, a million coupons. From the 4th quarter of 1994, by means of pursuing a strict monetary-credit policy by the National Bank, the exchange rate of the Coupon started gradual stabilization.

Massive "spreading" of coupons into circulation, when the economy was in fact not operating and the commodity deficit reached an extreme limit, gave rise to higher prices, devalued money and giving rise to deepening inflation. In the years 1992-1993-1994, the inflation rate increased from 300-400% up to 8000 percent.

Increasing the rate of devaluation of the Coupon from the beginning was supported by the fact that the Government could not establish the coupon as one of the means of taxation in the entire territory of the Republic. Parallel to this, US Dollars and Russian Rubles were being freely circulated in the country, which "occupied" the entire circulation of the Republic and the

Coupon had only 10% of circulation (when 60-65% of the entire circulation came from Russian Rubles and 20-25% from US Dollars). The Coupon was devalued in the way that among Soviet states, Georgia turned into the country with the most devalued currency: at the beginning of 1994 one Ukrainian Karbovanets equaled to 4.4 kopek, one reporting ruble of Belarus – 36 kopek, one Kazakh Tenge – 12 Rubles, one reporting Uzbek Manat – 30 kopek, one Azerbaijani Manat – 4 Rubles, one Armenian dram – 7.4 Rubles, one Kirgiz Som – 154 Rubles, one Moldovan Leu – 4.5 Rubles, one Turkmenistan manat – 601 Rubles, one coupon – 0.06 kopek (for information: when the April, 1993 coupon was involved, the coupon was one Ruble). Briefly saying, the Coupon, as a national banknote could not actually perform its obligations, functions, and purpose. If was, if fact, dead [44].

Of course, under the conditions of such devaluation of the Coupon, neither government, nor anybody else could pursue a highly effective monetary-credit policy. It was necessary to develop rapid activities and their pursuit in life to stop devaluation (fall) of the coupon, otherwise, industrial processes (respectively – political ones) were becoming unmanageable… and now, from the end of 1993, changing of the manager of National Bank began, as well as settlement of its activities, strengthening control of commercial banks and other credit establishments, deepening-widening relations established with the International Monetary Fund and World Bank, using their recommendations for improvement of the national Bank, and structures of the Ministry of Finance, rising taxes, strengthening supervisory functions of the activities of commercial banks and many others.

Consequently, since the 90s, a new stage begins in monetary credit policy and especially the National bank of Georgia. This is the period where reimplementation of monetary-credit policy begins, which is known in the name of the strict (or more adequate) monetary-credit policy.

The issue of replacing the coupon with a new currency became actual.

It shall be emphasized that experts in the International Monetary Fund and World Bank played an important role in determination of the role and image of the National Bank of Georgia, Ministry of Finance and other governmental structures, implementing current reforms in Georgia, their support and assistance.

The million times devalued Coupon counted its last days; replacing it with new banknotes was the request of the country and time.

Lari – Main State Attribute

On October 2, 1995, Georgian National Currency Lari was adopted, a sketch of which had been being created for two years by the State Commission. The name of the money was taken from “Vepkhistkaosani” (“The Knight in the Panther's Skin”), as a general collective name of property. As for the coins – Tetris, this was the name of Georgian money, silver coins in the 11th century.

Money reform is a harmful and complex process in any country. It shall serve for improvement of life levels of the population and an economic lift for the country with its strategic task and final purpose. Monetary reform may not be considered a simultaneous act, including replacement of a coupon of one kind with another. This is only one stage and is of a more technical nature. Solving the problem, including the essence of the monetary reform, is quite difficult and hardly an achievable task, which requires daily support and assistance from the side of the government and banks.

Before monetary reform, effective activities were implemented by the government of Georgia, the help of which achieved particular stabilization of the financial field. In more than one year before the Reform, balancing of the state budget at the expense of emission of money did not take place, supported greatly with liberalization of salaries, reformation of tax and custom systems, and acceleration of the privatization process. Monetary-credit policy was radically changed. Unjustified crediting of separate fields of industry through refinancing at the expense of money emission was overcome. Settlement between banks was based on the cash resources actually accrued on their accounts.

In the first part of 1994, strict restrictions were determined in the field of issuing cash money from deposits. At Tbilisi interbank exchange, operations were transferred to reasury operations for the purpose of stabilization of the official exchange rate. The Government continued issuance of payment debts, transferred to the banking system. Due to this, an independent market of cash free coupons was created, where the exchange rate was importantly lower than the exchange rate of cash money. Besides the fact, by implementing these activities, the fall of the official exchange rate was stopped before it destroyed trust of the population in the banking system. The Interbank credit auction was activated providing formation of real interest rates. The National Bank started implementation of necessary functions characterizing central banks of the country and in the first place, management of money masses existing in circulation. Transferring every account of budget to the National Bank removed the danger of taking additional money out of the budgetary channels, without control. At the same time, the National Bank didn't allow emission, which is definitely the result of monetary-credit policy. National Bank created a currency reserve, which made it possible to implement a flexible exchange rate policy at the Tbilisi Interbank Currency Exchange. By means of the implemented activities, the inflation rate was reduced to 9 percent in January, 1995; in February, March and April – to 3 percent, and starting from May – to one percent, i.e., the process of managing the financial system was started. Money mass was regulated, which was the outcome of work of the National Bank and general economic block of the Government. Economic stabilization gave essential change to the authority of the country in funding separate sectorial programs by the international monetary fund, World Bank, as well as the department of reserve and rehabilitation credits, EU reconstruction and development bank, and other credit institutions. Herewith, the phenomenon shall be noted that implementation of economic activities was attended by uncompromised fighting of the government in the direction of improvement of the criminology situation and establishing state order in every field of life.

The activities named above created real conditions for implementing monetary reform and involvement of national currency – Lari, which, in its turn, should create preconditions to recovery of production and improvement of life conditions of the population.

From September 25, 1995, bank notes of 1, 2, 5, 10, 20, 50 and 100 Lari and coins of 1, 2, 5, 10, 20 and 50 Tetris were issued to circulation. From October 2 of same year, Lari, which was divided into 100 Tetris, was recognized to be the only legal means of payment in the entire territory of Georgia.

Lari replaced the coupon from September 25 through October 2. The Exchange rate of coupon and Georgian Lari was determined at 1,000,000 (one million) to 1 (one). During this period, they stopped issuance of all kinds of banknotes from the accounts of legal entities and individuals existing at the banks and implementation of operations related with securities. Before October 2, coupons of the National Bank maintained the legal function of the means of payment together with Lari [40].

From September 25 till October 2, individuals and legal entities were given a warranty for exchanging Coupons held by them with Lari without any restriction in the amount. Exchanging coupons owned by people with Lari was implemented through the branches of the United Georgian Bank, while in the settlements, where the Bank had no representations, the exchange was provided as the temporary exchange of units formed by the managers of local authorities.

It was categorically prohibited to announce the exchange rate of foreign currencies. Exchange of foreign currency of one kind with the foreign currency of another should be implemented in National Currency – on the basis of cross-rate calculation subject to the announced rates on the information board for sale and purchase of foreign currencies. In case of violating the above mode, the National Bank immediately cancelled licenses of currency exchange units of the banking establishment.

At the first stage of involving Lari as the only means of payment, prices at the consumer market and not only there, for commodity products, were significantly increased. This fact, of course, put life conditions of empowered people much lower giving rise to dissatisfaction of the population.

This happened in about one week from involving Lari as the only payment instrument. During this period prices were increased in about 22-23 percent. In the subsequent period, the image was gradually changed and gradual stabilization of prices at the consumer market became evident. This process has not been slowed till today and though, it is hard to notice on daily basis, the trend of stability of prices is mostly expressed.

With monetary reform, Lari became necessary to perform all necessary functions characteristic to money. Including the most important function of saving Lari, in order to let the population, organizations and establishments trust in the force of Georgian currency, to place ones own savings in the banks not in the form of foreign currency, but in the form of the National Currency. It is most important to keep businessmen, business circles, enterprises and organizations, and citizens from problems in exchanging Lari with foreign currency, in order to prevent its discrimination. This could not be provided on the basis of credits of the World Bank for improvement of the situation; the economy should be activated.

By involving Lari, Georgia gained its principle state attribute – a National Monetary unit. This is truly the fact of epochal importance. For the purpose of involvement of national currency – Lari – into circulation, they developed the program for getting the Georgian economy out of the crisis, the most important priority of which was rapid restoration of the field of material production.

As it is known, Lari is the only legal means of payment in the territory of Georgia, except for cases foreseen by Georgian Legislation about free industrial zones. Only the National Bank is eligible to implement issuance of monetary symbols at the territory of Georgia. Therefore, the National Bank has exclusive right to produce monetary units for circulation or other purposes (commemorative).

The Board of the National Bank determines and approves the design of Banknotes and Coins (Tetris) of Lari, as well as their composition and other characteristics, after which the process of striking and minting the monetary units begin. Georgian money is being issued at the leading European organizations.

The National Bank provides transportation of ready monetary units to the territory of Georgia and their storage in the repositories of the National Bank. The population is provided with the monetary units through commercial banks.

After placing monetary units into circulation, natural process of their depreciation begins, which finally gives rise to their unfit condition for circulation. The average lifetime of the paper money is from 1 to 5 years, subject to the peculiarities of consumption. Coins remain in circulation for a much longer period. The National Bank provides systemic removal of unfit monetary units from circulation and their replacement with the respective amount of new coins and banknotes. Unfit monetary signs are exterminated according to the procedures prescribed by the Board of the National Bank.

The National Bank is the main expert in the issue of National Currency, and at the territory of Georgia – determination of authenticity of foreign currency and bank notes. It implements removal of counterfeit or falsified monetary units on a systemic basis. Therewith, extraction of counterfeit or falsified monetary units is provided without compensation.

Except for emission of the monetary units intended for circulation, National Bank is legally eligible to issue commemorative and investment coins of numismatic purpose [41].

Historic Importance of Involving the National Banknote

Involving a stable national currency was of great, decisive importance not only for the future faith of the monetary turnover of the country, but to the entire country, and implementing the hardest political, social and other transformation. National Bank started preparation for the involvement of Georgian Lari from the middle of 1994, when it made steps to stop the fall of the exchange rate of the Coupon. The first steps in this direction were made when a centralized report was transferred from the Ministry of Finance to the National Bank from July 1, 1994. Though this "rook" made particular problems to the part of outcomes of budget, the country started living in the regime of real incomes. At the same time, National Bank stopped issuance of nonguaranteed credits and emission money. From the same period, National Bank started strictly requesting performance of protection of 20% rate of so-called minimal reserves by the commercial banks, according to which these Banks should save 20% of attracted resources to the special accounts of the National Bank (later this rate was reduced more). Parallel to this, they activated such monetary mechanism as currency trades and credit auctions (from April, 1995), which the National Bank was participating systematically in and influenced essentially upon stabilization of the exchange rate of the Coupon through variation of its currency and credit intervention, extraction of its part from circulation and etc. Only in 1995, for the purpose of stabilization of the exchange rate of the Coupon, Tbilisi Interbank Foreign Exchange National Bank sold 55.2 million US Dollars and purchased 9.1 million US Dollars. Consequently, if at September of 1994 one US Dollar at the Black Market sold for 5-6 million Coupons, at the end of the same year, it cost 1.3 million Coupons. This conformity lasted almost till beginning the Reform – September of 1995.

If we take into account the fact that in the course of involving Georgian Lari, one Lari was exchanged on one million Coupons and its rate against the US Dollar was established to be USD 1 – GEL 1.3, which was maintained till September, 1998, it will become clear that the exchange rate of the National Currency was in fact reserved unchanged at one and the same marking, which spoke of huge work provided by the National Bank in implementation of monetary reform (of course, the monetary-credit policy of the national Bank could not do much for involvement of stable Georgian Lari, if not providing such other activities as sharp reduction of budgetary resources for maintenance of administrative units, synchronously to it cancelling subsidies on bread, electricity power, gas, liberalization of prices and later its entire release on numbers of products and many others).

After reaching a stable rate over a period of time (December, 1994 – September, 1995), the Government decided to implement monetary reform in the country and issue a new national currency – Lari instead of devalued Coupons, the amount of which in circulation was measured in trillions. Due to the fact that there was an unbelievable commodity deficit in the Country, it was necessary not only to issue new banknotes into circulation, but also to establish particular conformity between demand and distribution, and this could be implemented in the best and operative way by means of implementing reform in non-confiscation form, by sharp reduction of the money in circulation.

Preparatory works included organization of minting banknotes in France and then bringing them to Georgia. The National Bank solved the task successfully. It provided preparation of 801 million Laris (paper) and 600 tones of Tetris (coins) in France and brought them to Georgia, sorting and placing the respective pieces upon commencement of the Reform. From the side of the Bank, everything was ready for commencement of the Reform.

They decided to implement the Reform at the end of September. In this regard, on September 16, 1995, the General Republican Meeting was held at which representatives from every range of Government were invited, together with the leaders of local governments and law enforcement bodies, heads of banking and financial agencies, famous Georgian representatives of scientific and art domain and many others. Eduard Shevardnadze, giving a speech at the Meeting, declared that Georgian Lari would be entered into circulation from September 25.

Based on the Ordinance of the Head of the Government, the President of the National Bank N. Javakhishvili issued Ordinances No. 17 and No. 18 on September 18, 1995 on the Banking Ticket of the National Bank of Georgia on Putting Lari and Tetri Notes into Circulation and on Additional Activities of Exchanging Coupons with Lari. Regarding the Reform, the National Bank issued many other regulatory acts, letters and instructions (more than 60 in total). Huge organization works were conducted and within the prescribed terms (September 25 – October 2). Besides successfully exchanging old money (Coupon) with the new one (Lari), Lari obtained quite a high rate from the beginning. For example, if on the first day of involving Lari – September 25, one US Dollar cost one Lari and thirty Tetris, on December 18, 1995, one US Dollar cost one Lari and 24.5 Tetris…

For creation of a stable national monetary system and integral dominance of Lari in it, it was necessary to remove foreign banknotes (Ruble, US Dollar) from circulation, occupying a dominant place in money circulation of the Country. National Bank implemented this operation successfully: within the shortest period of time it removed from circulation 70.6 billion Rubles and 37.9 million US Dollars and created favorable circulation space for Lari.

After implementing the Reform, during almost three years, notwithstanding various hard internal and foreign economic and political, ethnic, social and other peripeteia, Lari maintained the same flag with its exchange rate, as it was determined upon commencement of the Reform (USD

1 = GEL 1.3). This was a great achievement. Thus, the National Bank gave to the country the strongest lever of "Archimedes" for reconstruction and development of the economy of the country, as well as its transfer to the market principles in the form of the National Currency of stable exchange rate – Lari.

DEVALUATION OF LARI IN 1998

The exchange rate of Lari, determined in course of the reform of 1995, was maintained over three years – till September, 1998, and made 1.3 Georgian Laris for 1 US Dollar, though stability of the exchange rate of Lari did not last long. In 1998, one international monetary financial phenomenon took place, which violated thr idyll of stability on the exchange rate of Georgian Lari instantly, and from September 5, 1998 its fall started and resulted in further devaluation.

The monetary-financial crisis suffered by Georgia, its national currency – Lari in September of 1998, started very far from its borders, in south-eastern Asia, in its industrially and financially highly developed countries: Hong Kong, Singapore, Taiwan, Thailand, South Korea, Malaysia, Indonesia, and Philippines. This Crisis was the most acutely suffered by South Korea, Thailand, Indonesia and Malaysia. In all these countries, in June of 1997, mass escape of capitals abroad took place, manufacturing rates fell, banks and other banking structures were bankrupted, exchange rates of currencies fell and their devaluations were one after another. Soon this crisis moved to Japan, then to Russia in August, 1998 and at the end of August of the same year, and the beginning of September, it reached Georgia.

Managing circles of leading western states, managers of the Monetary Fund and World Bank soon understood that if they would not operatively support the countries suffering monetary-financial crisis commenced in the countries of south-eastern Asia, the Crisis would be transferred to their countries with a "Domino Effect" (or the principle of connecting vessels), which would reach their countries and the same mistakes and outcomes would be repeated, which had taken place in 1929. When on September 12, 1929 the Crisis commenced in New York, the New York Stock Exchange was considered to be the Crisis of the USA, its "personal Case" and "did not move a finger" for supporting-localization of the Crisis, and as a result, it was soon said the Crisis was distributed in England, then to continental Europe, later in the whole world, ranging in the form of global crisis (great depression) over five years – 1929-1933. Besides the hardest financial-credit-monetary outcomes (budgets of all countries turned into deficits, more than 10,000 banks were bankrupted in the USA, currencies of every country were depreciated, their massive devaluation took place, etc.). The Global Crisis of 1929-1933 had the hardest social-political results: tens and hundreds of millions of people across the globe turned into an unemployed, impoverished, starving mass, giving rise to the favorable social "broth" for establishment of such dictatorships, as Mussolini in Italy, Hitler in Hungary, Francois in Spain, Salazar in Portugal, Port in Hungary, Horthy in Hungary and many others… and finally, the outbreak of the Second World War by the said Dictators and the countries managed by them, which cost the world 60 million dead people, more than 200 million wounded and disabled, 3.5 trillions of US Dollars, etc…

Foreseeing all the said events, western states implemented anti-crisis activities from the first days of the Crisis. To learn the situation and for the purpose of operative assistance, the Manager of the World Monetary Fund of those times, Michel Camdessus, traveled in the countries under Crisis; experts of other structures traveled and studied the situation in various countries and at the end of 1997 they adopted a multi-billion program of assistance of the countries suffering the Crisis, according to which, South Korea was granted a credit in the amount of 58.2 billion US Dollars, 42.3 billion US Dollars to Indonesia, 17.2 billion US Dollars to Thailand, etc. Credits were issued by the Monetary Fund, World Bank, USA, England, Germany, France, and Canada [45].

After receiving credits, the countries suffering crisis immediately devalued their currencies, cut expenditure parts of budgets, transformed manufacturing and banking systems, strengthened exports, reduced imports and as a result, soon, at the end of 1998, they received positive developments in economy, finances, banking field, and exchange rates of currencies.

Unfortunately, though devaluation (fall) of Georgian money (Lari) started from September 5, 1998 and continued till February, 1999 and was brought to 2.30 to 1 (one) US Dollar, though cheapening (devaluation) of Georgian money did not have favorable developments over the economy, production was not increased, exports were not extended and it did not give rise to the growth of reserves of foreign currency (US Dollar and others), etc. All these were and remain to be understandable: material and technical facilities of Georgian economy, its technologies, engineer thinking and management did not stand on the respective level (as in south-eastern countries), to provide a respective increase in output (for example, in 1995-1997 the growth rate of

Gross Domestic Product was 10%, though by taking into account the fact that starting point of growth equaled to zero, the said index of growth was really too low and it did not influence essentially or influence insignificantly upon movement of exchange rate of Georgian Lari) under the conditions of devaluation of Lari (cheapening production). Consequently, stagnation was developed in the Georgian economy, which, similar to the frozen age, continues till today.

Due to the fact that using the methods (increase in output, widening exports, cutting imports and many others) used in the south-eastern Asian countries for stabilization of their currencies, the government took the easy way for stopping the fall in the exchange rate of the Georgian Lari: it issued a maximally low amount of Laris into circulation and artificially increased demand on them. At last, this was made and is still being made at the expense of the population, at the expense of limiting consumption and worsening living conditions. This fact is confirmed with the fact that ridiculous rates were established: pensions – GEL 8 (later GEL 14), allowances – GEL 5, salaries – GEL 25-30 and many others, while the minimum wage was GEL 140-150.

Thus, devaluation of Georgian Lari, which started September 5, 1998 and continued till February, 1999 could not have any positive influence upon increase in output in Georgia; it was not being increased at all, or it was being increased so slowly and idly that they could neither influence the exchange rate of Georgian Lari, nor improve living conditions of the people...

Georgian Lari, involved instead of the Coupon, in September 1995 having a sufficiently high determined rate compared to the paralyzed, inactive state of the economy (USD 1 – GEL 1.30), was mostly maintaining the rate and stability at the expense of the widest layers of the population, (at the expense of worsening their living conditions, sharp reduction of their economic demand, at the expense of issuing a maximally low amount of money into circulation). This was provided through determining an extremely low rate of pensions, allowances to the refugees, scholarships for students, remunerations for employees and other payments (pension rate was GEL 8, allowances for refugees – GEL 5, scholarship – GEL 7, minimal remuneration – GEL 25-20, while the minimum wage was GEL 140-150). I.e., high rate and stability of Georgian Lari was maintained at the expense of massive impoverished, unbelievable "tightening of belts," and their starvation...

(Average annual index)

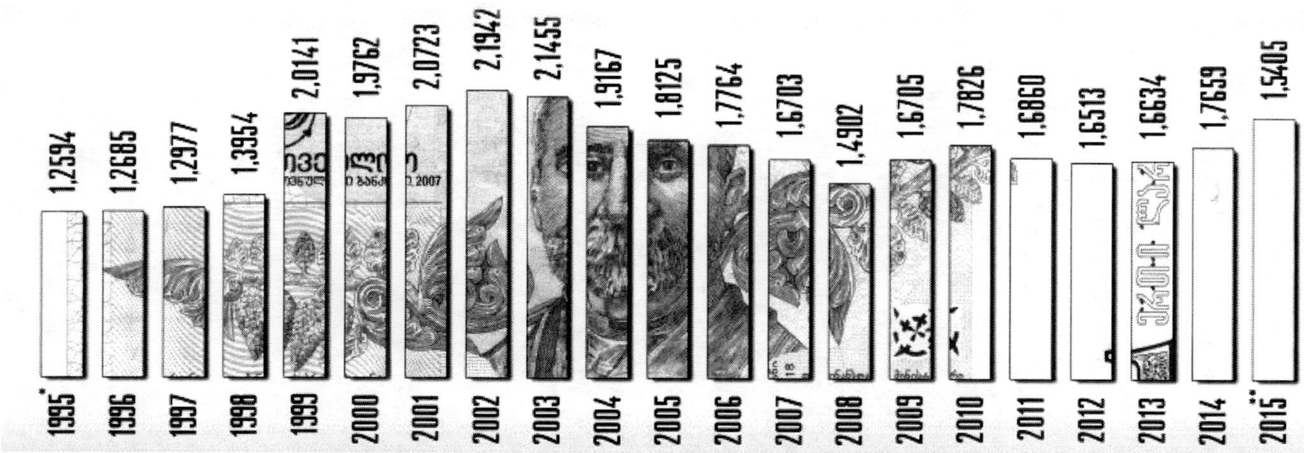

* - From September 25 through December 25

** - From January 1 through September 25

Chart 16. Exchange rate of Georgian Lari against US Dollars Years 1995-2015.

Prices are being increased incredibly in Georgia; growth is provided rapidly and in wide scales; living conditions of wide masses are being worsened, clearly increasing inflation is taking place, and at the same time the exchange rate of Georgian Lari is being proportionally increased, which is an incredible, unbelievable and mysterious phenomenon, a paradox, though it is the fact [41]. These words were written about events taking place in money circulation of Georgia in 1995-1998, by Professor Sh. Qiatauri. We may repeat the same evaluation after two decades in Georgia, at the edge of the 21st century

HISTORY OF MODERN GEORGIAN MONEY – COINS

Coins of 1, 2, 5, 10, 20 and 50 Tetri were put into circulation in 1995. Tetri, which was the name of one hundredth of Lari, is the Georgian monetary term established from the 13th century BC. The coins 1, 2, 5, 10 and 20 Tetris are of silver color, and 50 Tetri is golden. Authors of the design are: obverse – Elguja Amashukeli; reverse – Nodar and Bachana Malazonia. The National Bank of Georgia minted 10 Lari commemorative bi-metallic coins dedicated to the 2,000th anniversary of the birth of Christ and 3000 years of statehood of Georgia. The coins were circulated parallel to the banknotes of 10 Lari. The inner arc of bimetal coins is silver color, and the outer arch is golden. Ribs of both coins are engraved with the legends: "Georgia" and "Ten Lari," between the legends there are two stars imaged. Authors of the design are Emir Burjanadze and Tinatin Tevzadze.

National Bank of Georgia issued coins of 1 and 2 Lari and modified 50 Tetris. New coins were made of the newest technologies in the Mints of Austria, Holland and Great Britain. 50 Tetri coin of new modification will be in circulation parallel to old coin of same amount, and one and two Lari coins together with the paper money of respective amount. Authors of the design: Mamuka Gongadze and natia Dolidze.

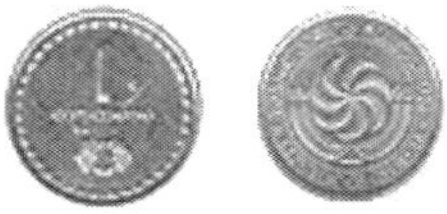

Year of mintage of one Tetri – 1993. Mass: 1.38 g. Diameter: 15 mm. Thickness: 1.25 mm. Composition: stainless steel – silver color.

Obverse: the denomination numeral "1" on the upper part of the coin, with the legend "თეთრი" (tetri) and the vine tendril underneath.

Reverse: The Borjgali (a Georgian symbol of the Sun with seven rotating wings) over the Christian Tree of Life, and the date of mintage, "1993," with

Georgian and English marginal legends on it, “საქართველოს რესპუბლიკა” and “REPUBLIC OF GEORGIA”

Year of mintage of two Tetris – 1993. Mass: 1.9 g. Diameter: 17.5 mm. Thickness: 1.25 mm. Composition: stainless steel – silver color.

Obverse: the peacock with spread wings on the upper part of the coin, with the legend “თეთრი” (tetri) and denomination numeral “2” underneath.

Reverse: The Borjgali (a Georgian symbol of the Sun with seven rotating wings) over the Christian Tree of Life, and the date of mintage, “1993,” with Georgian and English marginal legends on it, “საქართველოს რესპუბლიკა” and “REPUBLIC OF GEORGIA”

Year of mintage of five Tetris – 1993. Mass: 2.5 g. Diameter: 20 mm. Thickness: 1.32 mm. Composition: stainless steel – silver color.

Obverse: The golden statue of the lion from the 3rd millennium B.C. barrow of the Alazani valley, with the denomination numeral “5,” and the legend “თეთრი” (tetri) underneath.

Reverse: The Borjgali (a Georgian symbol of the Sun with seven rotating wings) over the Christian Tree of Life, and the date of mintage, “1993,” with Georgian and English marginal legends on it, “საქართველოს რესპუბლიკა” and “REPUBLIC OF GEORGIA”

Year of mintage of ten Tetris – 1993. Mass: 3 g. Diameter: 22 mm. Thickness: 1.27 mm. Composition: stainless steel – silver color.

Obverse: saint Mamai riding the lion, 11th century silver plate gilded with gold from the Gelati Monastery. The denomination numeral “10” on the right hand of the coin, and the legend “თეთრი” (tetri) underneath.

Reverse: the Borjgali (a Georgian symbol of the Sun with seven rotating wings) over the Christian Tree of Life, and the date of mintage, “1993,” with

Georgian and English marginal legends on it, "საქართველოს რესპუბლიკა" and "REPUBLIC OF GEORGIA"

Year of mintage of twenty Tetris – 1993. Mass: 5 g. Diameter: 25 mm. Thickness: 1.62 mm. Composition: stainless steel – silver color.

Obverse: the stag (adult male deer) from the painting of Niko Pirosmanashvili (Pirosmani), famous Georgian painter, with the denomination numeral "20" on the left-hand side, and the legend "თეთრი" (tetri) underneath.

Reverse: the Borjgali (a Georgian symbol of the Sun with seven rotating wings) over the Christian Tree of Life, and the date of mintage, "1993," with Georgian and English marginal legends on it, "საქართველოს რესპუბლიკა" and "REPUBLIC OF GEORGIA"

Year of mintage of fifty Tetris – 1993. Mass: 2.5 g. Diameter: 19 mm. Thickness: 1.4 mm. Composition: brass plated steel – golden.

Obverse: the relief of the Gryphon from the eastern facade of 11th century Samtavisi Cathedral, with the denomination numeral "50," and legend "თეთრი" (tetri) underneath.

Reverse: the Borjgali (a Georgian symbol of the Sun with seven rotating wings) over the Christian Tree of Life, and the date of mintage, "1993," with Georgian and English marginal legends on it, "საქართველოს რესპუბლიკა" and "REPUBLIC OF GEORGIA"

Year of mintage of ten Tetris – 2006. Mass: 6.5 g. Diameter: 24 mm. Composition: Copper-nickel – silver color.

Obverse: the coat of arms of Georgia surrounded with a symbolic image of Sun beams, the legends "საქართველო," and the date of issue "2006" under the coat of arms.

Reverse: the denomination numeral "50," and the legend "თეთრი" (tetri). There are microelements on both sides of the coin, analogue of ancient Colchis Tetri – Head of Lion. Milled. Bears a bilingual legend "საქართველო" and "Georgia," with five-pointed stars in between.

One Lari. Year of mintage – 2006. Mass: 7.8 g. Diameter: 26.2 mm. Composition: Copper-nickel – silver color.

Obverse: Half-milled. The coat of arms of Georgia, the legend "საქართველო" on the upper left side, and the date of issue "2006" on the lower right side.

Reverse: Half-milled. Denomination numeral "1" and legend "ლარი" (lari). Milled. Bears a bilingual legend "საქართველო" and "Georgia," with five-pointed stars in between. Both sides of the coin have a microelement – a lion's head similar to the one found on the old Colchian tetri coin.

Two Lari. Year of mintage – 2006. Mass: 8 g. Diameter: 27.0 mm. Composition: Inner ring: copper-aluminum-nickel alloy (gold color). Outer ring: copper-nickel alloy (silver color).

Obverse: the coat of arms of Georgia, the rim with a circular legend "საქართველო," and the date of issue "2006."

Reverse: denomination numeral "2" and legend "ლარი" (lari). The silver-color milled surface has an original design, representing a central symbolic image of sun rays. Both sides of the coin have a microelement – a lion's head similar to the one found on the old Colchian tetri coin. Milled. Bears a bilingual legend "საქართველო" and "Georgia," with five-pointed stars in between.

Ten Lari. Commemorative bi-metallic coin dedicated to the 2,000th anniversary of the birth of Christ. Year of mintage – 2000.

Mass: 10.6 g. Diameter: 26.0 mm. Composition: Inner ring: copper-nickel (silver color). Outer ring: copper-nickel-alloy (gold color).

Obverse: the obverse features a heraldic shield with crosses and the sacred gown of Christ in the center with the Georgian marginal legend: 2000 A.D.

Reverse: the reverse features the denomination numeral "10" with the inscription "ten" and "Lari." The edge is circled with the marginal legend that reads "NATIONAL BANK OF GEORGIA – 2000."

The edge of the coin is milled and bears a bilingual legend reading "საქართველო" "Georgia" and "ათი ლარი" "Ten Lari" with five-pointed stars in between.

Ten Lari. Commemorative bi-metallic coin dedicated to the 3,000th anniversary of Georgian statehood. Year of mintage – 2000. Mass: 10.6 g. Diameter: 26.0 mm. Composition: Inner ring: copper-nickel (silver color). Outer ring: copper-nickel-alloy (gold color).

Obverse: the obverse features bas-reliefs of the eagle and lion from the 11th century Svetitskhoveli cathedral (which signify the strength of the state). The composition is finalized by a leaf ornament and seven stars. The coin is circled with a legend that reads, in Georgian "3,000th Anniversary of Georgian Statehood"

Reverse: the reverse features the denomination numeral "10" with the inscription "Lari." The edge is circled with the marginal legend: "NATIONAL BANK OF GEORGIA – 2000."

The edge of the coin is milled and bears a bilingual legend reading "საქართველო" "Georgia" and "ათი ლარი" "Ten Lari" with five-pointed stars in between.

Source: National Bank of Georgia.

SUMMARIZING OPINIONS

In the beginning of the Manuscript, I said, in the form of a simply asked question: the main thing to me is to answer the question: how can we save Lari, economy, country… what shall we do?

Before summarizing the opinions of the economists given herein and my ideas, I will formulate modest suggestions and recommendations, answering my main question. I'd like to refer to the words of professor I. Archvadze: "entre nous, the greatest part of population does not care how and what proportion executive government and national bank share responsibility for inflation, exchange rate of Lari and volume and dynamics of domestic and foreign debts. – They want to leave in calm and stable environment, to have guaranteed job and progressing wealth.

This is a simple task at one glance, though still unachieved by most parts of the population of the country, as at the beginning of independence of Georgia, in the beginning of 1990s [29].

I agree with the first sentence of the professor. I will try to fade the pessimistic background of the second suggestion of the Author with my modest conclusions and suggestions; I will allow myself to try to give answers to the simply asked, but the most difficult questions, formulating reasons for revaluation of the monetary unit, and introduce you to my axioms of healing and strengthening the monetary unit of the country.

The Georgian economy and the Georgian monetary unit are to act under a complex global and regional environment. Under international globalization, relation of reproduction processes with such foreign factors as international trade, expert-import operations and real sector development is being strengthened, as well as foreign capital turnover, political stability, etc.

The unstable state of international relations and currency crisis may influence negatively upon economies of the country.

This is what has taken place in Georgia. Concussion and, moreover, canceling genesis of stability of the Georgian monetary unit was influenced by almost every factor of fluctuation and drop in the exchange rate of the currency. Subject to this, economic policy and especially, necessity of transformation of monetary-credit currency policy, becomes important.

It is of special importance to have economic growth, as well as wide scales of development of real sector. Only 0.03 percent of the global economy and 0.06 percent of the global population come from Georgia. In other words, Gross Domestic Product manufactured in Georgia is twice less per capita than average in the world. With the rate of economic growth of Georgia formed during recent years (2012-2015 – 4.6%), our country will not reach the level of Bulgaria with GDP produced per capital.

AXIOM 1. The problem of accelerating economic growth is of existent load and depends not only on the role and weight of the Georgian state, globally, but also its stability against domestic and external challenges, the level and dynamics of wealth of citizens and stability and, generally, existence of a Georgian monetary unit.

Panic formed at the international markets and Georgian Lari. Circumstances taking place in years 2014-2015, at the global and regional levels, made the Georgian economy face challenges, as the small and open economy of Georgia is quite vulnerable against foreign shocks. These phenomenon created a background of a strong foreign shock, reflected negatively upon the economy of the country from the point of reduction of inflow of foreign incomes.

Here, I'd like to emphasize situations created at the international markets, which were finally followed with the destruction of the exchange indexes at the leading international stock exchanges, reflecting on the monetary market of Georgia. The resonance, taking place at the monetary market of Georgia, is mostly conditioned with the panic created at the monetary market. Demand on the US Dollar has been significantly increased in Georgia, giving rise to the drop in Georgian Lari. To our mind, this is an extremely negative trend. Though such resonance is short-term and this process will be completed in a short period in Georgia, the resonance means the peak and we shall expect signs of stability in the near period.

I will give details about the phenomenon taking place in the global financial market.

During recent years, very interesting trends are reflected in the global economy. This is related with the extraordinary growth of Chinese economy, discussed by the international monetary fund in 2014, when it was the first to report that production of the National Economy in China, in one year, made 17.6 trillion US Dollars and almost overcame the US index. Though some experts calm themselves with the fact that this growth was provided with one amount, according to the GDP, and the USA is the leader, subject to the GDP. This, of course, was a new trend of development of the global economy and gave particularly reflected on the development of regional economies.

We shall assume that during the last period, when growth of the global economy was conditioned by an unbelievable growth rate of the Chinese economy, this would be naturally followed by particular changes, including the unforeseeable and crisis separated regions. This is the context we must consider the reality and datum formed during the recent period, which, in the first place, is related with appreciation of the US Dollar in relation with all other principle converted currencies and, on the other hand, in the global drop in prices on oil, which is the result of geopolitical changes, coming into particular dissonance with the trends of development of the global economy. At the same time, China is identified to be one of the partners of the western system and at the same time its competitor. Result to this are the changes taking place in the international arena and echoes of which are heard in the regions again. With this point of view, the example of 'Black Monday' at the stock exchange of China is the clearest example, when a significant drop in indexes took place. Naturally, this influences upon our country as well, though lightly, as the degree of integration of our economy in the global economy is so low that it cannot have any serious or essential influence upon trends taking place in the economy of Georgia.

AXIOM 2. Notwithstanding the above, it is necessary to understand sustainability of the Georgian economy in connection with any expected economic threats faced by the country;

Cheapening oil. In course of speaking about reasons for devaluation of Georgian Lari, we shall foresee the global and regional environment that the Georgian economy is operating in. Out of the external shocks influencing it, we shall emphasize the sharp reduction of oil prices. As importers of oil, Georgia finds direct benefit from low prices of oil, as money wasted in the business is reduced, though this benefit is covered by the influence of a hard recession and strong devaluation of Russian currency upon the region. The sharp drop in oil prices became a heavy load to the oil-producing countries in the region, such as Azerbaijan and Kazakhstan. This gave rise to the reduction of money entering with exports in about 20-25%.

Oil prices continue to cheapen in the global market. During the last month (July of 2015), the oil price was reduced 23.3%. One of the main reasons for such reduction in prices is complete removal of economic sanctions to Iran. According to the Minister of Oil of Iran, Mr. Bijan Namdar Zanganes, Iran intends to increase oil production, even if this takes place at the expense of dropping prices. The US position coincides that of Iran. According to the US Institute of Oil, the United States of America, under such conditions, doesn't think of reducing production, moreover, production has been increased by two million barrels during the last weeks.

Notwithstanding the fact that there is a higher trend of reduction in the global market, the processes taking place globally is not reflected at the market of Georgian fuel. If during last one month the price has dropped in 23.3% in the world, none of the companies has reduced prices in Georgia, except Gulf, which reduced prices by 5 Tetris, only on diesel. As appealing with the exchange rate of the National Currency, in such case, oil companies will not get use of it, as the national currency will be stabilized (but at the high marking of devaluation). According to the latest data, reduction in prices in the global market are more than 23%; as for Georgian market, these prices are not being changed there."

AXIOM 3. To overcome cardinal changes, financial and currency cataclysms, and social-economic risks, it is necessary to process long-term state programs where there will be creation of increasing economy. Every expected financial risk of financial outcomes (i.e., cheapening oil, appreciation of US Dollars, etc.), macro-economic environment of the country, the banking sector and circumstances taking place in it, their strategy and management, global standards of development and future perspectives will be analyzed.

Appreciation of US Dollar positions. In the first part of 2014 and 2015, parallel to the positive economic trends and expectations in the USA, the US Dollar started appreciation. This was accompanied with announcement of decisions of the US Federal Reserve System about leaving the policy of quantitative easing and strengthening the monetary policy, which appreciated positions of US Dollar.

Consequently, most monetary units of the world faced important devaluation. Strengthening the US Dollar is important to Georgia from the point that in the three main trading partner countries of Georgia (Turkey, Russia, Ukraine) significant devaluation of local currencies against the US dollar took place; therewith, their economic trends were pressured. It is not new that the Georgian economy greatly depends on the degree of stability of the economy of neighboring countries. 52% of imported goods to Georgia come from 52% of CIS states. Under such conditions, we bring economic instability, inflation and devaluated currency from the trading countries.

Thus, main place in the risks of prognosis for Gross Domestic Products is occupied by the foreign sector. Particularly, at the background of the geopolitical tension, if the economic crisis becomes deeper than expected, or trade partner countries of the region or/and if the said shock is transferred to Georgia more than expected, economic growth will be reduced compared to the prognosis. On the other hand, if agreement of free trading with Europe and large investment projects is reflected on the economic growth larger than expected, or business sentiment is improved more than expected, GDP growth will be higher than prognosis.

AXIOM 4. If more money exits the country than enters, this gives rise to economic fluctuations. Georgia shall gradually get out of the dollarization system, but many people think it to be better if the mass of US Dollar is reduced in the country. Today, we have ugly financial forms from the financial point of view: for example, settlement, tax collection, and issuance of salary is provided in Georgian Lari, but when it comes to savings, we prefer US Dollars. Due to the fact that our life is related with US Dollar, its sharp reduction influences negatively upon exchange rate of Georgian Lari. According to the experts, getting out of dollarization may be provided only with particular financial balances and moreover, with development of local production.

Low level of localization of economy. Since 2010, National Bank has been being actively working towards growth of effectiveness of monetary policy; the main preventing factor is low level of localization of economy of Georgia. Under the condition of high dollarization the mechanism of transferring the interest rate is weakened, as an important part of supplying money to the economy is provided in foreign currency, on which interest rates are determined by central banks of other countries in compliance with economic cycles existing at their countries and it goes beyond the field of control of the National Bank. Under the conditions of low localization, changing the exchange rate transfers to inflation, preventing flexibility of exchange rate. Besides this, in the course of low Larization risk of exchange rate is important for economic agents unsafe from fluctuation of the rate, especially to the borrowers of banks, whose incomes are denominated in national currency, and loan is taken in foreign currency. In such case credit risk of portfolio of commercial banks is increased, which is conditioned with the misbalance of the creditors' currencies, i.e., currency induced credit risk. Consequently, change in the exchange rate of Georgian Lari against US Dollar may influence seriously upon the credit portfolio of commercial banks.

AXIOM 5. One of the objectives of the National Bank is increasing Larization. The continuous Larization process is noteworthy, as changing behavior of economic agent requires existence of a developed financial market and sustainable economic stability during the years.

Export of the country. Deficit of current account. Economic and political developments were reflected in export processes of Georgia. Incomes made from exports implemented in direction to the main export markets, in fact, were reduced to the historical minimum. The current account deficit in the first part of 2015 was increased to 14.9% and the worsening was mostly conditioned with 27.7% reduction in export of goods. The sharp pace of export reduction started in the fourth quarter of 2014. Together with the export, money transfers (27.3%) and incomes made from tourism were reduced as well (2.9%). In turn, the annual growth of imports, which was positive in the fourth quarter of last year, became negative in the first quarter of the current year and made 3.3%. It is also noteworthy that the rate of import reduction is being increased during last periods, which speaks of activation of the process of import correction of the reduced monetary incomes and supports macroeconomic stability. I considered it to be purposeful to refer to the review of the Prime Minister of the Country: "nothing special is taking place in Georgia; on the contrary, we have overcome this stage. More than 300 million US Dollars have left the country; misbalance between export-import is eliminated as well and we have no fundamental problems at current stage" [30].

AXIOM 6. We consider assistance of export to be urgent objective, as well as development of local production. Strengthening growth of Lari production or devaluation with reduction of production is a real image reflecting the state of Georgian economy. I consider it a positive decision to have replacing products at the local market. This will influence positively upon the exchange rate of Georgian Lari, as we will not need additional US Dollar for purchasing imported products. Moreover, it is not difficult to use weak national currency for using local production.

The factor of foreign debt is extremely noteworthy, to evaluate the national monetary unit and in this particular case – Georgian Lari. It is not a secret that starting from 2008, during the following 4 years National Currency greatly depended on the foreign debt and not the real state of the economy. If we add to this growth of the volume of foreign debt of the country, it appears that stability of National Currency through 2012 partially depends on the foreign debt and not the real state of the economy. Since 2013, Georgia stopped taking on new debt. This was a kind of shock, as we were accustomed when we had less US Dollars, we used to take loans and everything was regulated; we held Lari firmly in our hands. Today this factor is removed and the exchange rate of Georgian Lari has "run away." I'd better say that exchange rate of Georgian Lari was released from artificial brakes.

Though, taking foreign debt is provided in slow pace. State budget takes foreign debt and grants of more volume than it pays foreign debt and respectfully, due to devaluation of exchange rate, by means of converting, much more funds are entering than leaving the budget.

AXIOM 7. It is necessary, imminent and possible to raise foreign debt in foreign currency from the international financial organizations, governments of foreign countries and institutions of commercial projects by Georgia. Main thing is to determine the amount of foreign capital, which may be mastered by the country, the amount of debt to be served by the government of provided country, if respective criteria of the parameters of foreign debt are protected and the main foreign debt should be used purposefully and effectively.

Investments are one of the main ways of moving towards sustainable development of Georgian economy. It is not only necessary to attract foreign investments, the most important thing is to direct the mechanism of implementing investment strategy towards internal investment of the country and new investment projects, as well as their practical use.

They will blame me to be maximalist for these words, but I will write it anyway: at the background of financial crisis existing in Georgia, I consider investments to be if not the only, but one of the main drivers for economic growth, economic strength, or even economic survival and solving financial or social problems of the country. The facts that there is a small amount of domestic resources based on economic development, limited budgetary resources and small savings of economic subjects for investments in Georgia make me say these words.

Generally, playing important role in solving objectives of investment development of the country, for inflow of investments into the country and respectively strengthening rate of Georgian Lari is impossible with self-regulation of such market, which is distinguished in low level of formation in our economy. We consider it necessary to strengthen the role of government, correction of economic policy, and searching for optimal conformity of governmental and basic regulations. Therewith, limits and principles of participation of government in the investment process shall be determined, based on the specificity of economic development of Georgia characterizing the period of transferring to the market.

For helping Georgian Lari, the Government adopted and implemented the plan of realization in an accelerated mode of privatization objects. Therewith, investments of record volume entered the country last year compared to the last seven years. Even under these conditions, Georgian Lari continued devaluation. Both forwarded steps are the attempts of solving problems in the short-term perspective. It is impossible to let such a huge flow of investments from privatization and foreign investors, which may stop the fall of Georgian Lari.

AXIOM 8. Activation of the investment policy of the government under modern conditions is the main term for transferring Georgia to sustainable economic development. It will be impossible to speak about improvement of the index of economic growth without an important investment boom in Georgia. Sharp amplitude of fluctuation of Georgian Lari will be balanced only when each Tetri from privatization and millions of investments entering Georgia is used in a stalled real sector, used for material production and development of agriculture; as a result, people will be employed, they will have incomes, local products will manufactured, we will not leave with imports, we will sell ours and inflow of cash funds will be started from exports.

The increasing role of the banking sector in formation of the economy and image of the country. When there is a global trend of increasing rates of Georgian Lari and when currencies of every main trading partner of Georgia is falling against the US Dollar, Georgian Lari would not be left in initial condition. I say this to create the opinion about monetary policy of the national Bank.

By the way, I do not agree with such sharp separation, but they distinguish two principle regulators of the Georgian economy: monetary-credit policy – is the prerogative of national bank; as for the monetary provision, it is borne by the governmental structures.

Monetary policy of the National Bank influences distribution of credits in the economy (though I can say nothing negative about issuing credit); the main objective of the National Bank is to provide stability of prices. At the same time, National Bank shall provide stability and transparency of the financial system and assist sustainable economic growth in the country by way of preventing performance of its principle objective. Another thing is that in course of determining monetary policy, National Bank is based on the targeting of inflation. Successful functioning of targeting the mode of inflation (activated in 2009 in Georgia) includes particular terms and conditions.

Special importance in the process of formulating decisions of monetary policy is granted to forward looking inflation, as changing instruments of monetary policy by the National Bank is transferred to the economy with particular time sequence and it influences upon future inflation. The long-term targeted index of inflation of the National Bank is 3 percent. Thus, striving of the National Bank towards the established norm of inflation shall be considered to be justified.

The factor preventing growth of effectiveness of monetary policy of National Bank is the low level of Larization in Georgia. Though during 2014, the growth of Larization index of deposits and loans was stipulated, due to the uncertain nature of the exchange rate of Georgian Lari this growth was modest. In case of the deposits, Larization index was improved 1.7 percent and made 39.8 percent; in case of loans, it was increased 3.3 percent up to 39.2 percent (excluding effect of changing exchange rate).

The mode of a floating exchange rate is working in Georgia, which is considered to be the most optimal regime of exchange rate for the open economies of such small size, as Georgia's. For such economies, floating exchange rates fulfill function absorbing shocks. In such case, changing the exchange rate weakens the negative influence of the said shock upon the real economy – economic growth and inflation.

Herewith, existence of the exchange rate conditioned with the mode of targeting is determined with the strategy of monetary policy of the National Bank of Georgia. Under the conditions of a floating exchange rate, determining the exchange rate takes place according to the demand-distribution existing at the monetary market, which, in turn, is influenced by the fundamental economic factors and temporary phenomenon. Under the said mode, the currency market is characterized with short-term fluctuations. Such fluctuations are bigger in the counties of similar small and open economies of high dollarization, related with a small volume of currency market and unstable flows of capital. Monetary policy of the National Bank foresees intervention through currency auctions at the currency market only under particular conditions: if temporary inflow of excess capital takes place, giving rise to sharp short-term fluctuation of the exchange rate for filling international reserves and balancing state foreign operations.

Today, for some reason, everybody, who knows much, or who knows little or knows nothing about these issues, considers every mechanism of monetary policy (targeting, floating exchange rate, enclosing negative index of inflation with the purposeful one, loans of refinancing, depository certificates of national bank, treasury obligations of government or loan bonds) in the negative context of the activities of the National Bank. Moreover, anti-deflation policy of the National Bank should be the policy supporting of fall of the exchange rate of Georgian Lari.

AXIOM 9. Fluctuation of exchange rate of Georgian Lari shall be, in the first place, purposeful, with market mechanisms, and on the other hand – it shall be implemented for avoidance of important losses. In the first place, it is necessary to neutralize inflation expectations, negative expectations. Here, coordinated work of the government and national bank is necessary.

Once again about budget. It is extremely important to maintain the trend of equal spending. It is extremely important to maintain an equal spending trend of budget. Budget was being spent unequally for almost decades in Georgia; this happened in the second quarter of 2014. Worsening deficit of current account pressured Georgian Lari and it played an important role on devaluation of Georgian Lari.

We shall allocate a positive side as well: in 2015, the budget of the country is already being equally wasted. The Ministry of Finance is trying to accumulate balance. At this stage, the Ministry of Finance has accumulated more than 800 million Georgian Laris, which is a serious factor supporting the exchange rate. Probably, this index will be increased up to 1 billion, which will also influence positively upon the exchange rate of Georgian Lari.

AXIOM 10. Extremely important is the influence of budgetary expenditures upon devaluation of Georgian Lari. This includes disciplined management of budgetary expenditures and their equal distribution till the end of the year, also to cut current expenditures to a maximal extent and to have basic orientation towards a real economy and creation of infrastructure in the country.

Conclusion

National Bank and the executive government shall work synchronically. Two main issues shall be decided in a formalized, accelerated way: together with strengthening monetary policy, the National Bank shall provide measured currency interventions; executive government shall attract and develop first tranches of grants and credits foreseen in the budget of 2015 in a maximally timely manner. Implementation of monetary and fiscal policies shall be implemented in unison, in order to make successive steps as by the Ministry of Finance, so National Bank and thus must assist avoidance of stability and inflation within the short-term period:

- The main thing is diagnosis, to be made by the government. It shall have accurate uptake of the task and in such case, decisions may be respective. Ministry of Economy, National Bank, Ministry of Finance and respective agencies shall work together to the direction guarantying irreversible process; everything shall be made to recover currency inflow, to have high economic growth, expressed in the growth of real incomes.
- Unfortunately there is no other receipt (?!).
- Improvement, development of mechanism of export promotion shall be implemented within shortest terms;
- Activities shall be pursued at the target markets – this, in the first place is monitoring of portfolio existed in direction of infrastructure and, on the other hand, planning scheduled projects, in order to implement additional projects, and promote the economy.
- Every hasty adopted restriction shall be cancelled;

- We shall wait to see how the budget is fulfilled and how newly formed negative factors in currency inflow are eliminated:
  - Drop in export;
  - Reducing incomes from tourism;
  - Reduction in railway and other transportations;
  - Reduction in transfers;
  - Increasing outflow of money abroad.
- Cycle of reforms shall be processed and concluded, stimulating and creating mechanisms and preconditions for attraction of long-term investments, Georgian Lari will not simply stand such incompetence.
- Changes shall be started from the Tax Code and they shall be completed with the mechanisms, which are approved in the developed countries.
- Inflation control shall be provided at the expense of economic growth, when it maintains artificial prices – deficit and price of production is not changed. Shall not an entrepreneur have motivation for working?
- Government intended stabilization of situation from the sums accepted from the monetary fund, there is logic – entering currency in cash would partially improve balance of demand-delivery at the currency markets and later would prevent or alleviate devaluation. Though, this is a single event and such process would not have been stopped. Today's problems would be "shifted" until full spending of borrowed or gifted money,
- It is necessary to increase income in maximal extent, which is a direct responsibility of the government, will not increase export potential of the country (how can we do it? L.Q.), but work may be provided to the mechanism of promoting exports.
- Inflation expectation may be worse than the inflation itself, because inflation expectation is excess load and pressure on Georgian Lari. In such case, notwithstanding the fact that if the bank client needs currency or not, he keeps purchasing it for some reason and this gives rise to the negative results.
- For the purpose of maintaining purposeful index of inflation during middle-term period, National Bank of Georgia shall activate instruments of monetary policy in 2015-2017: refinancing loans, depository certificates, operations with governmental securities, currency interventions, standing instruments, minimal reserve requirements, etc.

- Currency conduct of large trade-partner states of Georgia shall be studied and parallels shall be made in relation with Georgian Lari, of course, for pursuing correct monetary policy.
- We shall set the essential task to increase exports, we can even make use of the weakness of the National currency in some cases and replace imports with local production. Otherwise, we shall continue living in virtual reality, take new debts, etc.
- To do everything for recovering currency inflow, have high economic growth, which, of course, is expressed in growth of incomes.
- Unfortunately, there is no other receipt.
- Under such conditions, it is necessary to have one fundamental value: the exchange rate of the National Currency shall be determined at the open market! The rate formed at open and non-speculative markets and under such conditions, shall be accepted by the government and population as an objective scheme.

APPENDIX 1. EVERYBODY SHALL WORK TOGETHER

Several decades ago, Israel's financial system faced huge problems, as the Shekel was catastrophically devalued; neighbors turned into the enemies of the country and imposed economic sanctions. Notwithstanding this, after a year and a half, Israel could overcome every problem.

They could not print zeros to Shekels; the economy was getting worse day by day; prices reached fantastically high levels; massive dismissal of officials took place; huge queues appeared at the shops – frightened people tried to make reserves of products until prices got higher.

In 1984, after the Lebanon War of 1982, the Arab states imposed economic sanctions against Israel; this was added with increasing prices on oil and a terrible crisis was started in Israel. They named reduction of the level of taxes on imported goods as the reason for the economic fall, and it destroyed the Israel market and local production. This was accompanied by distribution of allowance and social assistance by politicians, and foreign debt of the country reached astronomic size. Though, in a year and a half, the Country could get out of the crisis and today the Shekel is among the top 17 converted currencies worldwide.

The Country could do this due to the fact that the government explained clearly to people, if they did not tighten belts, soon the US Dollar would cost a billion Shekels. - This is how Jerusalem economist Natan Rabin explained the above period. – Therewith, the officials understood well that you cannot take people's wealth continuously, as finally all these will be followed with manifestations and riots. Due to this, to counterbalance unpopular measures in the population, the Government refused massive dismissal of employees working at the public sector. They froze prices on food – the Government threatened owners of shop and farmers who dared create deficits of food or speculation of products with imprisonment. Consequently, the people had hope that, even in case of development of situation in the worst scenario, their children would not be hungry and homeless.

After this, the era of "universal restrictions" was started: Israel Minister of Finance Yitzhak Moda'I was called "Mr. Have not" – this is the answer he used to give everybody who asked him for money. They reduced pensions in the country; young mothers were obliged to return to jobs four days after childbirth; they taxed every luxury item, such as apartments, cars, TV-sets, jewelry and… even excess consumption of fuel by the owners of private vehicles. Notwithstanding the hard crisis with professional unions, they reduced salaries, especially in agriculture, in order to cheapen products and through this to make them more popular abroad and to promote better sales Europe and United States of America, and thus the country would receive more currency. At the same time, credits became cheaper for the farmers, and it was the time when they started growing strawberries and other fruit and vegetables in the waterless desert, which had been imported from Arab states and the cost was very expensive.

It's evident that these reforms were not approved by everybody. They blamed economists in the attempts of destruction of Israel and connection with enemies, though positive fluctuations took place gradually.

It is noteworthy that in many counties such "brutal policy" was followed by overthrow of the governments and protest rallies, but Israel could persuade people to "wait for a while." It didn't take long: inflation of 1985 increased only 20 percent, the gap in the budget was filled, and thus it was not necessary any more to reduce salaries to the public officials. In 1985, denomination of the Shekel took place – one New Shekel equaled to 1000 old. After that, during multiple years, one US Dollar costs 3-4 Shekels. Those times, they threw tons of mud at the Minister of Finance of Israel Mr. Yitzhak Moda'I, on the other hand, future economists from different parts of the world are learning his experience at the universities.

APPENDIX 2. SAMPLES OF GEORGIAN MONEY IN DIFFERENT ERAS

ასი მანეთი
100
CENT ROUBLES
AYANT COURS OBLIGATOIRE
AU MÊME TITRE QUE LES BILLETS
DE CREDIT RUSSE
100
СТО РУБЛЕЙ
ИМѢЕТЪ ХОЖДЕНІЕ
НАРАВНѢ СЪ РОССІЙСКИМИ
КРЕДИТНЫМИ БИЛЕТАМИ
100
100
100
100

სამი მანეთი
3
3
TROIS ROUBLES
AYANT COURS
OBLIGATOIRE AU
MÊME TITRE QUE LES
BILLETS DE CREDIT
RUSSE
ТРИ РУБЛЯ
ИМѢЕТЪ ХОЖДЕ-
НІЕ НАРАВНѢ СЪ
РОССІЙСКИМИ
КРЕДИТНЫМИ
БИЛЕТАМИ

1919

ხუთასი 500 მანეთი
ხუთასი 500 მანეთი

ხუთი მანეთი
ბონი
საქართველოს რესპუბლიკისა
1919

Ancient Georgian Coins

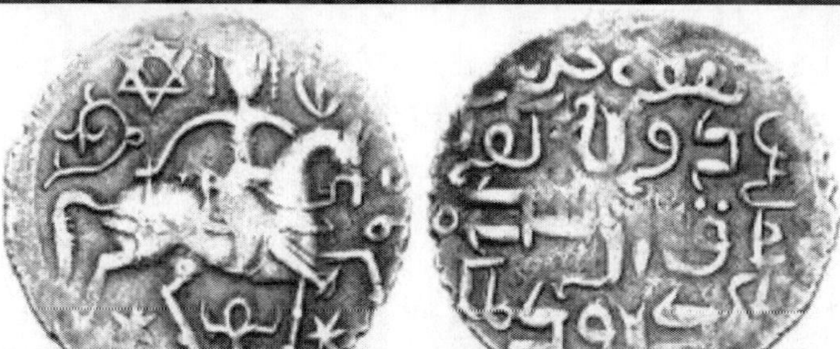

GEORGIAN MONEY OF THE 90S – COUPON

1000

250

1000

500000

REFERENCES

[1] *Annual Report of the National Bank of Georgia*, 2014. Tb.: National Bank of Georgia. pg. 8.

[2] Javakhishvili, N. 2015. During Monetary Crisis, National Bank Increased Volume of Georgian Lari in the Economy. This Was Main Reason or Devaluation of the National Currency/Banks and Finances www.BFM.ge #397, March, pg. 5.

[3] IMF, WEO Update, Jan-2015.

[4] BRD (Regional Economic Prospects, Jan-2015) and IMF assessment (WEO Update, Jan-2015).

[5] EBRD Evaluation. *Regional Economic Prospects*, Jan-2015.

[6] EBRD Evaluation. *Regional Economic Prospects*, Jan-2015.

[7] EBRD Evaluation. *Regional Economic Prospects*, Jan-2015.

[8] Chichinadze, N. 2015 75% of Gross Foreign Debt of the Country Was Taken in 2006-2012/Banks and Finances, #395, February, pg. 3.

[9] Basilia, T. 2015. Is not this the subject the government should be interested in?/SaqarTvelos Respublika, No. 120, July 1. Pg. 2.

[10] Pavliashvili, S. 2015. How Exchange Rate of Georgian Lari Is Influenced by Petrol Mafia/Premieri, February 19-25, No. 05(071), pg. 8.

[11] Sadikovi, A. 2015, It Was Impossible to Avoid Devaluation of Lari. www.BFM.ge. #395, pg. 5. Financial.news.ge.

[12] Eliava, L. National Bank, in Fact, Plays with Georgian Population/Banks and Finances. #400. March, www.BFM.ge.

[13] Martadze, L. 2015. New Wave of Devaluation of Georgian Lari Is the Result of the Policy of National Bank. www.BFM.ge. #398, pg. 3.

[14] Gotsiridze, R. 2015. What Will Happen With Georgian Lari? Premieri. No. 02(068) January 299 – February 4. pg. 14.

[15] Javakhishvili, N. 2015. Who Plays with Georgian Lari? Kviris Palitra. March 23, pg. 8.

[16] Center of Analyze and Prognosis of Tbilisi State University Relates Devaluation of Lari with Inadequate Decision of the National Bank/Banks and Finances. #413. June. pg. 8.

[17] Khomizurashvili, V. 2015. Exchange Rate Fluctuation is a Normal Phenomenon, though These Changes shall not be in One Direction/Banks and Finances. #401. April, pg. 9.

[18] Griffiths, M. Processes Related with Exchange Rate of Lari Entirely Depends on External Factors/Banks and Finances. #397. pg. 2.

[19] Silagadze, A. 2045. Only "Tightening Belts" Will Not Be Enough For Crisis Overcoming/Kviris Palitra, March 15.

[20] Toqmajishvili, M. 2015. Why Is Lari Predicted to Have Hard Autumn/Kviris Palitra, August 10-16. pg. 33.

[21] National Bank of Georgia. Annual Report. 2014. pg. 31-32.

[22] JSC Partnership Fund. About Us; Investment Activities.

[23] Kovzanadze, I. 2015. Partnership Fund will Provide Market in 2015 150 Million US Dollars in the Form of Capital. www.BFM.ge. #408. May. pg. 9.

[24] Quistauri, L. 2015. Opportunities for Influencing Exchange Rate of Lari with Monetary Instruments. www.BGM.ge. #418. July. pg. 3.

[25] Basilia, T. 2015. Present State of Banking Sector Does not Allow Positive Assessment of the Supervisory Service. www.BFM.ge. #419. August, pg. 3.

[26] Kalandadze, L. 2015. Currency Machinations in the Country of "Winged Angels"/Saqartvelos Respublika, No. 98, May 30, pg. 3.

[27] Namchadze, B. 2026. According to Nodar Khaduri, Budgetary Costs Have not Give Rise to Devaluation of Lari/Premieri. FactCheck. February 12-18. pg. 22.

[28] Archvadze, I. 2015. In Search of the Protagonist of Devaluation of Georgian Lari / Saqartvelos Respublika, March 21. pg. 9.

[29] Gharibashvili, I. 2015. Expressed Speculation and Resonance Takes Place in Connection with Exchange Rate of Lari/Saqartvelos Respublika, August 26, No. 159. pg. 2.

[30] Chichinadze, N. 2015. National Bank Fails to Fulfill Requirements of the Monetary Fund. www.BFM.ge<http://www.BFM.ge> #419. August, pg. 5.

[31] Kakulia, M. 2015. Speculative Transactions are Noted between Banks at the Currency Market, www.BFM.ge<http://www.BFM.ge> #394. pg. 3.
[32] Meskha, I. 2015. Social-Economic Reforms in Georgia: Reality and Challenges. Works of the Academy of Economic Science of Georgia. No. 12, Tb.: Universali, pg. 62.
[33] Chichinadze, N. 2015. The Myth of Safety of Refinancing Loans. www.BFM.ge No. 401. April. pg. 3.
[34] National Bank of Georgia. 2015. Inflation Review. July.
[35] https://ka.wikipedia.org/wiki.
[36] The Georgian Chronicles, 1955. Vol. I; pg. 40; Javakhishvili Iv. 1925. Georgian Measurements Knowledge i.e., Numismatics – Metrology, Tbilisi; Kapanadze, D. 1950; Georgian Numismatics, pg. 25-40.
[37] Chantladze, V. 1987. History of Money, Credit and Finances (Section Four); Money, Credit and Finances in Georgia (Section One). Lecture Course for the Students of Economic Faculty. Tbilisi, pg. 95.
[38] https://burusi.wordpress.com/2010/03/30/rezonans/.
[39] Bakhtadze, L. Kakulia, R. Kandelakishvili, L. 20?? Modern Money and Money Circulation. Manual. pg. 318.
[40] Anguridze, O. Charaa, V. Dogonadze, I. 2015. Security Problems & Modern Challengers of the Georgian National Currency. TSU. Center for Analysis and Forecast. g. 54.
[41] Qistauri, Sh. 1993. National Currency (Past, Present, Future). Tbilisi. pg. 80.
[42] Newspaper "*Bank*," 1993, March 13.
[43] Qistauri, L. 1996. *National Bank* (Formation, Activity, Future). Tbilisi; pg. 76-80.
[44] Fedyakina, P.N. 2005. *International Finances*. M., pg. 450 (in Russian).

ABOUT THE AUTHOR

Lamara Qoqiauri
Director of the English Language Advanced Study Private School
and Founder and director of nongovernmental organization -
"Fund of Financial-Investment Policy and Strategy" (FFIPS).
Academic Affiliation: Doctor of Economic Science, Professor,
Member of the Academy of Economic Sciences of Georgia
and Scientific Academy of New York.
lqoqiauri@yahoo.com

Finished Tbilisi School of Physics and Mathematics named after Komarov; graduated from the Faculty of Economy at Tbilisi Iv. Javakhishvili State University. Under the tutorship of Vasil Chantladze in 1986 passed Ph.D. defense. In 2003, she defended doctoral dissertation on the topic "Formation and Development of Investment market in Georgia" and was conferred professor's degree.

Published 232 scientific manuscripts, mostly on finances, banks and investments, including 21 monographs and 20 manuals. Basic manuscript: "Investment market: Theory, Policy, Practice". Tb.: Publishing company "Siakhle", 2002; Investment Management and Policy, in 2 volumes. Tb.: 2008; Theoretical Genesis of Investments, New York, USA. 2009; Fundamentals of Banking. Third edition. Tb.: STU. 2010; Intellectual Capital, Herausgeber, TU Bergakademie Freiberg, Germany. 2013 and etc.

She began working with specialization during studentship from the first course – at National Bank of Georgia; in 1978-2008, she worked at Tbilisi State University as a professor. In 2009-2015, she worked as full professor at Technical University of Georgia. She was elected for the True Member of the Academy of Economic Sciences and New York Academy of Science.

Along with her principle activities, in 1992 she established and continues management of the first English Language Advanced Study Private School. She found also nongovernmental organization - "Fund of Financial-Investment Policy and Strategy" (FFIPS).

INDEX

#

21st century, 87

A

Abkhazia, 75
access, 34
age, 85
agencies, 82, 103
agriculture, x, 14, 39, 43, 44, 72, 100, 108
amplitude, 100
anemia, 53
Armenia, 6, 8, 9, 15, 19, 20, 35, 66
Armenians, 65
Asia, 65, 83
Asian countries, 85
assessment, 6, 14, 33, 117
assets, 2, 16, 24, 29, 30, 38, 48, 51
Austria, 87
authenticity, 80
authorities, 49
authority, 66, 72, 78
avoidance, x, 3, 23, 102, 103
axiom, xiii, 45, 46, 50
Azerbaijan, 6, 8, 9, 10, 14, 15, 19, 20, 21, 66, 96

B

backwardness, 7
banking, xiii, 14, 29, 46, 47, 49, 50, 53, 54, 58, 59, 60, 77, 79, 82, 83, 84, 96, 100
banking sector, 14, 29, 47, 50, 53, 58, 59, 60, 96, 100
banks, 33, 44, 45, 46, 50, 55, 56, 57, 58, 59, 60, 72, 75, 76, 77, 78, 79, 83, 84, 97, 121
barley, xi
barter, 61, 62
basis points, 58
beams, 89
Belarus, 76
beneficiaries, 39
blame, 45, 49, 53, 55, 99
bonds, 19, 29, 102
borrowers, 53, 97
bounds, 9, 20, 34, 39
brass, 89
budget deficit, 75
budgetary resources, 81, 99
Bulgaria, 8, 9, 94
bureaucracy, 36
business environment, 36
businesses, x, xiii, 45, 46

C

capital input, 38
cash, ix, 6, 7, 17, 20, 21, 22, 26, 33, 35, 51, 56, 59, 77, 100, 104
cash flow, ix
catering units, xi
central bank, xi, 7, 49, 77, 97
Central Europe, 19
challenges, 19, 51, 94
children, 108
China, 5, 8, 9, 14, 15, 43, 44, 62, 63, 95
Christian symbol, 66
circulation, 1, 34, 35, 51, 52, 65, 66, 72, 74, 75, 77, 78, 79, 80, 81, 82, 85, 87
CIS, 14, 15, 17, 97
cities, 62
citizens, 19, 53, 54, 73, 79, 94
civil war, 72, 75
civilization, 61
climate, vii, viii, xi, 4, 46
cocoa, 62
color, 87, 88, 89, 90, 91
commerce, 1
commercial, 2, 34, 40, 44, 47, 48, 51, 53, 56, 57, 58, 62, 63, 64, 66, 76, 80, 81, 97, 99
commercial bank, 34, 40, 44, 47, 51, 53, 56, 57, 58, 76, 80, 81, 97
commodity, 2, 3, 4, 17, 18, 67, 72, 75, 79, 81
communication, 14, 34
compensation, 80
competition, 35, 46, 50
compliance, 97
composition, 80, 91
conditioning, 25, 49
conflict, 6, 16, 19, 20
conformity, 31, 34, 39, 49, 81, 99
consolidation, 38, 39, 47
construction, xi, 13
Consumer Price Index, 5
consumers, 53
consumption, 67, 80, 85, 108
copper, 15, 61, 62, 63, 64, 65, 66, 67, 68, 90, 91
corn, xi, 4
correlation(s), 38, 39, 50
cost, 58, 59, 65, 66, 75, 81, 82, 84, 107, 108
counsel, x
counter measures, 55
counterbalance, 107
credit rating, 47
creditors, 39, 59, 98
crop insurance, 39
crop(s), xi, 39
culture, 67
currency, vii, xi, xiii, 1, 2, 3, 6, 7, 8, 10, 11, 20, 23, 25, 26, 29, 30, 32, 33, 34, 35, 40, 43, 49, 50, 51, 52, 53, 55, 56, 60, 63, 71, 72, 73, 74, 76, 78, 79, 80, 81, 83, 84, 94, 95, 96, 97, 98, 99, 101, 103, 104, 105, 108
current account, 11, 12, 14, 15, 18, 23, 24, 98, 102
current account deficit, 98
current prices, 47

D

Dagestan, 66
danger, 3, 34, 39, 53, 59, 78
debt service, 59
debts, 27, 29, 39, 56, 59, 77, 93, 105
defects, 67
deficit, 11, 13, 14, 15, 18, 23, 24, 25, 27, 38, 50, 51, 57, 58, 75, 81, 102, 104
deflation, 2, 102
demonstrations, 74
deposits, 59, 77, 101
depreciation, xi, 2, 9, 80
depression, 83
depth, 33
derivatives, 16, 24, 30
destruction, 74, 94, 108
destructive process, 34
devaluation, vii, ix, xi, xiii, 2, 3, 6, 7, 8, 9, 10, 16, 19, 23, 26, 30, 31, 32, 33, 36, 39, 40, 45, 49, 50, 52, 53, 55, 57, 72, 74, 75,

76, 83, 84, 85, 95, 96, 98, 99, 100, 102, 104
developed countries, 56, 83, 104
developing countries, ix, 2, 3, 33
diplomacy, 1
direct foreign investment, 13, 18, 24, 46
direct investment, 14, 16, 23, 30, 46
disability, 26
disappointment, 3
discrimination, 79
dissatisfaction, 79
dissonance, 95
distribution, 55, 74, 81, 100, 101, 102, 107
domestic demand, 32, 38
domestic investment, 47
domestic resources, 46, 99
dominance, 82
donors, 25
dream, 51

E

economic activity, 3, 5
economic crisis, 97
economic cycle, 97
economic development, x, xi, 45, 46, 49, 65, 67, 73, 99, 100
economic growth, xi, 2, 3, 6, 7, 16, 39, 43, 45, 46, 51, 53, 94, 97, 99, 100, 101, 103, 104, 105
economic independence, 39
economic policy, 26, 37, 38, 39, 49, 94, 99
economic problem, 23
economic relations, 6, 66
economics, 43
economy, vii, viii, ix, x, xi, xiii, 1, 2, 3, 4, 5, 6, 7, 10, 19, 20, 22, 23, 25, 26, 27, 29, 32, 33, 34, 35, 36, 37, 38, 39, 40, 43, 44, 45, 46, 47, 48, 49, 50, 51, 53, 55, 56, 57, 59, 65, 72, 74, 75, 79, 83, 84, 85, 93, 94, 95, 96, 97, 98, 99, 100, 101, 102, 103, 107
education, x
effective exchange rate, 32
Egypt, 65
electricity, 81
emission, 33, 63, 71, 77, 78, 80, 81
employees, 74, 85, 107
employment, 44, 46
enemies, 107, 108
energy, 4, 6, 10, 17, 47, 48
England, 72, 83, 84
English Language, 121, 122
entrepreneurs, 45
environment, xi, xiii, 46, 93, 95, 96
Europe, 6, 19, 20, 41, 63, 83, 97, 108
European Union, 15, 17, 31
excess supply, 4, 54
exchange rate, v, vii, viii, ix, x, xi, 1, 2, 3, 7, 8, 25, 26, 27, 29, 32, 33, 34, 35, 40, 41, 45, 49, 50, 51, 52, 54, 55, 56, 57, 58, 74, 75, 77, 79, 80, 81, 82, 83, 84, 85, 87, 93, 94, 96, 97, 98, 99, 101, 102, 105, 117, 118
exchange rate policy, 78
execution, 40
expenditure policy, 40
expenditures, 5, 33, 38, 39, 44, 45, 50, 51, 59, 62, 102
export market, 20, 21, 98
export promotion, 103
exports, vii, 2, 8, 15, 16, 17, 20, 23, 26, 40, 56, 84, 85, 96, 98, 100, 104, 105
external shocks, 95
extraction, 80, 81

F

faith, vii, 49, 80
farmers, x, xi, 108
Federal Reserve, 7, 19, 96
feelings, 31
fertilizers, 15
financial, xiii, 1, 3, 7, 23, 24, 26, 29, 30, 43, 46, 48, 50, 51, 52, 53, 54, 56, 58, 60, 62, 72, 77, 78, 82, 83, 84, 94, 96, 97, 98, 99, 100, 107
financial crisis, xiii, 3, 56, 60, 83, 99
financial markets, 43
financial resources, 46

financial stability, 52, 54
financial system, 3, 62, 78, 100, 107
fiscal policy, v, vii, viii, xi, 5, 37, 49, 50
fish, 66
flexibility, 97
floating exchange rates, 101
fluctuations, 3, 9, 30, 36, 41, 53, 97, 101, 108
food, xi, 3, 4, 107
force, 46, 79
foreign banks, 59
foreign debt, v, viii, ix, 25, 26, 27, 28, 29, 39, 44, 60, 93, 98, 99, 107, 117
foreign direct investment, 46
foreign exchange, xiii
foreign investment(s), vii, xi, 13, 18, 24, 44, 46, 47, 99
foreign investors, viii, 45
formation, 27, 49, 52, 56, 72, 77, 99, 100
France, 6, 72, 82, 84
funding, 13, 15, 18, 23, 24, 33, 39, 48, 52, 59, 73, 78
funds, 37, 45, 46, 51, 55, 57, 59, 63, 72, 99, 100

G

Georgia, vii, viii, ix, x, xii, xiii, 2, 3, 4, 6, 7, 8, 9, 10, 11, 12, 13, 14, 15, 16, 18, 19, 20, 21, 22, 23, 24, 25, 26, 27, 29, 31, 32, 33, 34, 35, 37, 38, 39, 40, 44, 45, 46, 47, 48, 49, 50, 51, 53, 54, 55, 56, 57, 58, 60, 64, 65, 66, 67, 68, 69, 70, 71, 72, 73, 74, 76, 77, 78, 79, 80, 82, 83, 85, 87, 89, 90, 91, 93, 94, 95, 96, 97, 98, 99, 100, 101, 102, 104, 105, 117, 118, 119, 121
Georgian Economy, v, viii, 43
Georgian farmers, x
Georgian Lari, v, vii, viii, ix, x, xi, xiii, 1, 2, 3, 7, 8, 9, 10, 23, 25, 26, 27, 29, 30, 31, 32, 33, 34, 35, 37, 38, 39, 40, 41, 43, 45, 49, 50, 51, 52, 53, 54, 55, 56, 57, 58, 73, 78, 80, 81, 82, 83, 85, 86, 87, 94, 95, 97, 98, 99, 100, 101, 102, 104, 105, 117, 118
Georgian monetary unit, vii, xiii, 40, 56, 93, 94
Georgians, 64, 71
Germany, 6, 8, 9, 61, 66, 72, 84, 121
gifted, 104
global demand, 4
global economy, 1, 4, 94, 95
globalization, 1, 93
God, 69
goods and services, 11, 16, 19
governments, 57, 99, 108
graduate students, 73
grants, 26, 37, 99, 103
Great Britain, 14, 40, 87
Greece, 6, 17, 20, 25
Greeks, 66, 67
Gross Domestic Product (GDP), 4, 5, 6, 7, 11, 12, 14, 16, 23, 29, 30, 32, 38, 39, 43, 44, 46, 47, 52, 85, 94, 95, 97
growth, 2, 3, 6, 11, 12, 13, 14, 15, 18, 20, 21, 22, 23, 25, 27, 29, 32, 35, 39, 40, 45, 46, 50, 51, 52, 53, 58, 72, 75, 84, 87, 94, 95, 97, 98, 101, 103, 105
growth rate, 12, 84, 95
guilty, 44
gunpowder, 68

H

hard currency, 54
healing, x, 93
hermaphrodite, 68
high school, xiii
history, 26, 55, 61, 65
Hong Kong, 83
hostility, xi
hotels, xi
human, 61, 68
Hungary, 84
hunting, 61, 68
hyperinflation, 63

I

identification, vii, x, 34
image(s), 11, 14, 58, 64, 65, 67, 68, 76, 79, 89, 90, 98, 100
IMF, 4, 117
imported products, 31, 98
imports, 2, 3, 17, 30, 31, 33, 56, 84, 85, 98, 100, 105
imprisonment, 108
inadmissible, 31
income, 12, 13, 19, 33, 39, 53, 58, 104
independence, 25, 50, 68, 71, 73, 93
individuals, 33, 78
Indonesia, 83, 84
industrial environments, 51
industrial relations, 1
industry, x, xi, 14, 19, 43, 44, 51, 72, 77
inevitability, vii, xi
inflation, vii, ix, xiii, 2, 3, 4, 5, 6, 7, 30, 31, 32, 45, 51, 52, 55, 56, 58, 72, 75, 78, 87, 93, 97, 101, 102, 103, 104, 108
infrastructure, xi, 37, 44, 47, 48, 102, 103
institutions, 46, 54, 78, 99
integration, 95
interbank market, 35, 56, 57
interest rates, 32, 44, 46, 59, 77, 97
interference, 33
international financial institutions, 48
international investment, 29
International Monetary Fund, x, xii, 3, 4, 5, 6, 40, 72, 74, 76
International Partnership Fund of Georgia, xii
international relations, 1, 94
international standards, 54
international trade, 1, 93
intervention, 34, 35, 50, 81, 101
investment climate, vii, viii, xi, 46
investment projects, vii, xi, 47, 48, 97, 99
investment(s), vii, viii, xi, xiii, 4, 7, 13, 14, 16, 17, 18, 24, 26, 29, 30, 34, 36, 45, 46, 47, 48, 49, 51, 56, 73, 80, 97, 99, 100, 104, 121
investors, xi, xiii, 3, 6, 47, 48, 52, 100
Iran, 12, 69, 96
Ireland, 6
Israel, 73, 107, 108
issues, vii, ix, xiii, 37, 40, 53, 57, 59, 74, 101, 103
Italy, 6, 8, 9, 17, 20, 84

J

Japan, 3, 8, 9, 73, 83
judiciary, 72
justification, 73

K

Kakhetians, 65
Kartli, 64, 66, 68, 69, 70
Kazakhstan, 8, 15, 96
Korea, 83
Kutaisi, 70

L

law enforcement, 82
laws, xi
learning, 108
lease payments, 33
Lebanon, 107
legend, 65, 66, 87, 88, 89, 90, 91
legislation, 44
liberalization, 45, 77, 81
lifetime, 80
light, 66
Lion, 90
liquidity, 51, 57, 58
livestock, 67
living conditions, 85, 87
loans, 2, 14, 26, 29, 31, 32, 33, 36, 44, 46, 47, 48, 49, 51, 52, 53, 54, 57, 58, 59, 99, 101, 102, 104
local authorities, 79
local government, 82
localization, 52, 83, 97
logistics, 48

long-term debt, 18
lying, 68

M

magazines, 73
Malaysia, 83
management, viii, 47, 48, 50, 52, 54, 57, 60, 72, 74, 77, 84, 96, 102, 122
manufacturing, 83, 84
market economy, 50
market share, 4
market-oriented economy, ix
mass, 23, 26, 33, 34, 40, 50, 51, 52, 57, 59, 72, 78, 83, 84, 97
materials, x, 75
measurement, 62
media, xii, 27, 54, 73, 74
medical, 15
metals, 3, 4, 5, 62, 67
Middle East, 35, 64
military, 6, 10, 20, 75
mineral water, 15
minimum wage, 85
monetary, vii, viii, ix, xi, xiii, 1, 2, 3, 5, 6, 7, 8, 9, 14, 19, 32, 33, 36, 37, 40, 43, 44, 51, 52, 54, 56, 57, 58, 59, 60, 61, 63, 71, 72, 75, 76, 77, 78, 79, 80, 81, 82, 83, 87, 93, 94, 95, 96, 97, 98, 100, 101, 103, 104, 105
monetary market, 7, 94, 101
monetary policy, 4, 7, 8, 19, 32, 33, 40, 54, 57, 58, 96, 97, 100, 101, 103, 104, 105
monetary-credit policy, ix, 37, 60, 75, 76, 78, 81, 100
Mongols, 69, 70
motivation, 104
multiple factors, 31

N

naming, 73
national bank, ix, x, xii, 2, 3, 9, 12, 13, 16, 18, 21, 22, 24, 29, 31, 32, 33, 34, 35, 36, 37, 38, 40, 44, 45, 47, 49, 51, 52, 53, 54, 56, 57, 58, 59, 60, 71, 75, 76, 77, 78, 79, 80, 81, 82, 83, 87, 91, 97, 98, 100, 101, 102, 103, 104, 117, 118, 119, 121
national currency, vii, xi, xiii, 1, 8, 10, 25, 26, 32, 40, 43, 49, 51, 73, 74, 78, 79, 80, 81, 83, 96, 97, 98
national debt, 25
national product, 44, 53
National Service of Statistics of Georgia, x, xii
negative outcomes, 55
Netherlands, 14
New York Stock Exchange, 83
nickel, 89, 90, 91

O

official exchange rate, 77
officials, 107
oil, 2, 3, 4, 5, 6, 7, 17, 19, 20, 31, 43, 95, 96, 107
oil production, 4, 43, 96
open economy, 19, 94
operations, xiii, 1, 11, 26, 59, 77, 78, 93, 101, 104
opportunities, 20, 36, 45, 46, 52, 56, 62
optimization, 45
ores, 66

P

paper money, 63, 71, 80, 87
parallel, 11, 19, 87, 96
parity, 53
parliament, 49, 60
petroleum, 14
Philippines, 83
pipeline, 14
Pirosmanashvili, Niko, 89
playing, 23, 99
Poland, 12

policy, ix, xi, 1, 6, 7, 19, 32, 33, 36, 37, 45, 46, 50, 53, 54, 58, 60, 75, 76, 77, 78, 81, 94, 96, 100, 101, 102, 104, 108
population, 9, 55, 56, 74, 77, 78, 79, 80, 85, 93, 94, 105, 107
portfolio, 14, 24, 30, 48, 97, 103
portfolio investment, 14, 24
Portugal, 84
preparation, 14, 80, 82
president, 3, 33, 51, 53, 74, 82
prevention, vii, 52
principles, 49, 55, 83, 99
private investment, 48
private ownership, 36
private sector, 29, 36
privatization, 37, 44, 77, 100
probability, 35
producers, 53
professionalism, 35, 57
professionals, 55
profit, 13, 39, 44, 46, 47, 58
profit margin, 39
prognosis, 4, 6, 31, 32, 40, 55, 97
project, 48, 49
propaganda, 55
protection, 81
public officials, 108
public sector, 107
publishing, viii, 74

R

raw materials, 5, 43
reading, 91
real estate, 4, 5, 14, 48
real income, 5, 6, 81, 103
reality, 26, 53, 55, 58, 95, 105
recall, 53
recession, 6, 39, 95
recognition, ix
recommendations, vii, xi, 53, 76, 93
reconstruction, 78, 83
recovery, 35, 78
reform(s), 47, 73, 76, 77, 78, 79, 81, 82, 83, 104, 108
refugees, 85
regional economies, 95
regulations, 16, 20, 47, 49, 50, 53, 99
rehabilitation, 78
reliability, 31, 66
relief, 89
reproduction, 1, 93
requirements, 49, 53, 54, 104
researchers, x
reserve assets, 30
reserves, 3, 27, 29, 34, 37, 44, 52, 60, 81, 84, 101, 107
resources, 23, 26, 46, 48, 52, 57, 58, 77, 81
restoration, 79
restrictions, 40, 77, 108
retail, 33
retardation, 43
revaluation, 93
risk management, 54
risk(s), 7, 19, 31, 32, 41, 47, 51, 52, 53, 54, 96, 97
Romania, 8, 9
root, vii
ruble, 76
rules, 47, 50, 56, 66
Russia, 4, 6, 7, 8, 9, 10, 12, 13, 15, 16, 17, 18, 19, 20, 21, 31, 35, 40, 60, 66, 74, 83, 96

S

safety, 47, 72
sanctions, 6, 19, 96, 107
Saqstati, xii
savings, 46, 55, 79, 97, 99
scholarship, 85
science, x
Second World, 63, 84
securities, 58, 63, 78, 104
security, 50
segregation, 37
self-regulation, 99
sellers, 56
services, 11, 12, 15, 23
settlements, 78

shape, 68
shareholders, 47
Shevardnadze, Eduard, 74, 82
shock, 19, 26, 38, 41, 52, 94, 97, 99, 101
short-term interest rate, 57
signs, 6, 30, 33, 62, 63, 68, 80, 94
silver, 62, 64, 65, 66, 70, 77, 87, 88, 89, 90, 91
simulation, 44
Singapore, 83
slaves, 62
social construct, 74
social life, 74
social problems, 99
society, 34
solution, xiii, 31
South Korea, 73, 83, 84
sowing, 39
Spain, 6, 20, 84
specialization, 121
speculation, 33, 108
speech, 82
spending, 51, 102, 104
stability, 3, 9, 26, 27, 29, 34, 37, 38, 44, 45, 47, 49, 52, 53, 59, 60, 79, 83, 85, 93, 94, 97, 98, 99, 100, 103
stabilization, 4, 10, 16, 34, 54, 75, 77, 79, 81, 85, 104
stars, 87, 90, 91
starvation, 53, 85
state enterprises, 29
statehood, 64, 87, 91
state(s), 1, 2, 4, 8, 10, 14, 15, 16, 17, 25, 26, 29, 35, 36, 38, 39, 44, 46, 49, 51, 54, 56, 59, 65, 66, 67, 71, 72, 73, 74, 76, 77, 78, 79, 83, 84, 85, 91, 94, 96, 97, 98, 101, 105, 107, 108
statistics, 26, 29, 30
steel, 87, 88, 89
stimulation, 51, 63
stock, 44, 94, 95
stock exchange, 44, 94, 95
storage, 67, 80
stress, 6, 75
structure, 26, 46
style, 68
Sun, 87, 88, 89
supervision, 47, 50
suppliers, 31
survival, xiii, 99
sustainability, viii, 3, 48, 95
sustainable development, 99
sustainable economic growth, 100
sustainable growth, x, xiii
Sweden, 66
symbolism, 68

T

Taiwan, 83
target, 2, 7, 103
tariff, 72
tax collection, 97
tax deficit, v, viii, 11
tax system, 63
taxation, 74, 75
taxes, 45, 76, 107
Tbilisi, 40, 69, 70, 77, 81, 118, 119, 121
teachers, x, xiii
teams, 48
technologies, 84, 87
telephone, 74
tension, 97
territory, 61, 64, 67, 69, 70, 75, 78, 79, 80
Thailand, 83, 84
threats, 95
tones, 82
tourism, 13, 22, 23, 44, 48, 98, 104
trade, 4, 6, 7, 8, 11, 13, 23, 26, 55, 97, 105
trade deficit, 7, 11, 13
trading partners, 19, 20
tranches, 37, 103
transactions, 55, 56, 63
transformation, ix, 1, 39, 62, 80, 94
transparency, 100
transport, 12, 14, 23, 47
transportation, 63, 67, 80
Turkey, 7, 8, 9, 10, 12, 15, 17, 18, 21, 31, 96
Turkmenistan, 76

turnover, 48, 64, 71, 80, 93
turtle, 68

U

Ukraine, 4, 6, 7, 8, 9, 10, 12, 13, 15, 17, 18, 20, 21, 96
unions, 108
United Kingdom, 4
United States (USA), 3, 4, 5, 7, 8, 9, 15, 17, 19, 21, 72, 83, 84, 95, 96, 108, 121
universities, 108
USSR, 74

V

vegetables, x, 108
vehicles, 15, 108
versatility, vii
vessels, 83

W

war, 60, 63, 75
weakness, 105
wealth, 44, 93, 94, 107
Western countries, 74
wheat, xi
workers, xiii, 13, 73
World Bank, x, xii, 74, 76, 78, 79, 83, 84
worldwide, 43, 56, 107

Y

Yeltsin, Boris, 74

Z

Zhordania, Noe, 71